AUSTRALIAN WRITERS

HENRY HANDEL RICHARDSON

Von allem Geschriebenen liebe ich nur das, was einer mit seinem Blute schreibt. Schreibe mit Blut: und du wirst erfahren, daß Blut Geist ist … Furchtbar ist das Alleinsein mit dem Richter und Rächer des eignen Gesetzes.

Nietzsche, *Also sprach Zarathustra*

OXFORD

AUSTRALIAN WRITERS

HENRY HANDEL RICHARDSON

MICHAEL ACKLAND

Melbourne

OXFORD UNIVERSITY PRESS

Oxford Auckland New York

OXFORD UNIVERSITY PRESS AUSTRALIA
Oxford New York
Athens Auckland Bangkok Bombay
Calcutta Cape Town Dar es Salaam Karachi
Kuala Lumpur Madras Madrid Melbourne
Mexico City Nairobi Paris Singapore
Taipei Tokyo Toronto
and associated companies in Berlin Ibadan
OXFORD is a trade mark of Oxford University Press

First published 1996

National Library of Australia
Cataloguing-in-Publication data:

Ackland, Michael, 1951– .
Henry Handel Richardson.
Bibliography.
ISBN 0 19 553 764 5.
1. Richardson, Henry Handel, 1870–1946—Criticism and interpretation. I. Title. (Series: Australian writers (Melbourne, Vic.)).

A823.2

Typeset by Desktop Concepts P/L, Melbourne
Printed through Bookpac Production Services, Singapore
Published by Oxford University Press,
253 Normanby Road, South Melbourne, Australia

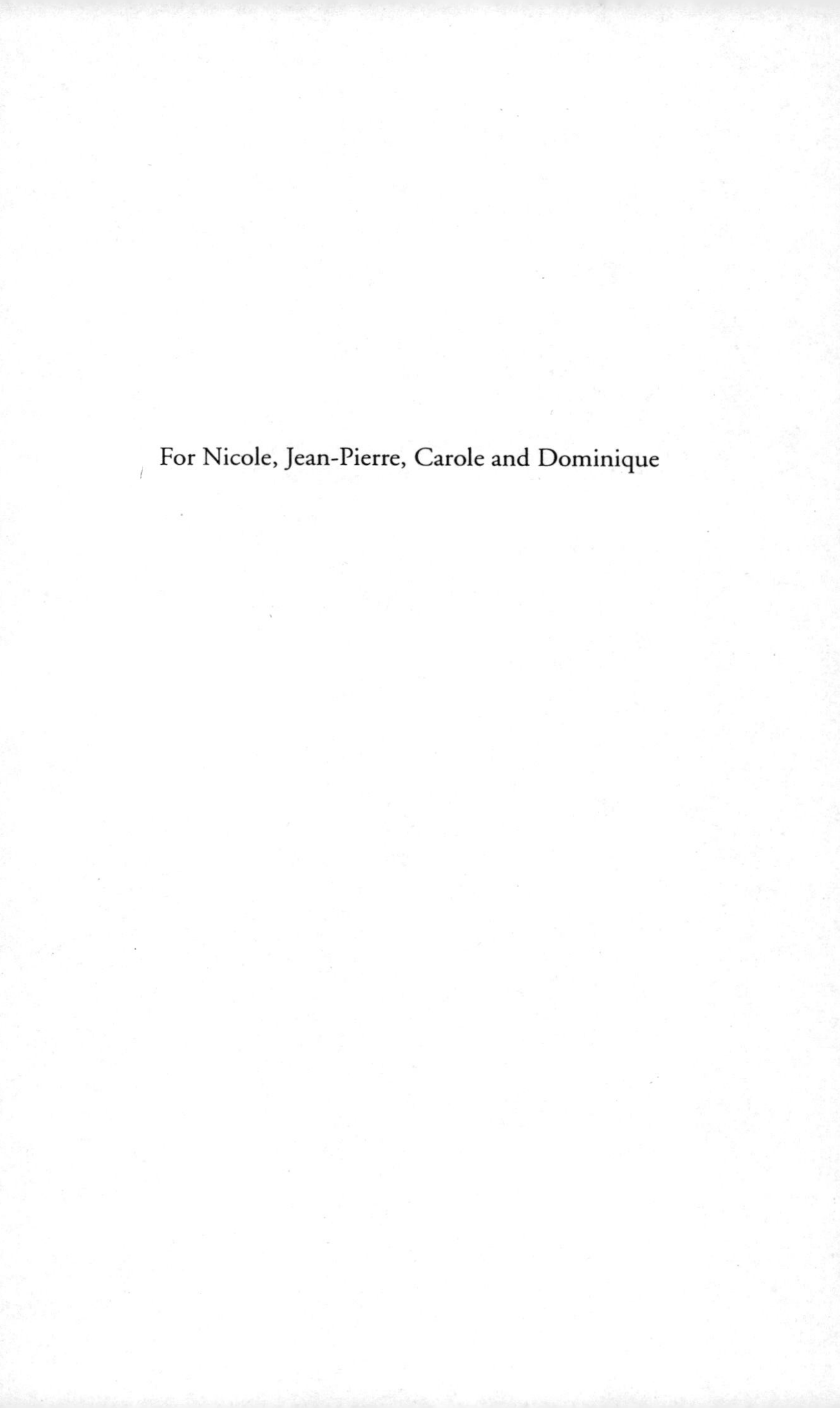

For Nicole, Jean-Pierre, Carole and Dominique

CONTENTS

A Note on Texts and Abbreviations

Page references from Richardson's work are identified by abbreviations to the following texts:

EC — *The End of a Childhood and Other Stories* (Heinemann, London, 1934)

GW — *The Getting of Wisdom*, new edition (Heinemann, London, 1931)

MG — *Maurice Guest* (Heinemann, London, 1908)

MWY — *Myself When Young* (Heinemann, London, 1948)

RM — *The Fortunes of Richard Mahony* (Heinemann, London, 1930)

S — 'The Coat' and 'Sister Ann', *Southerly*, 23, 1 (1963)

YC — *The Young Cosima* (London: Heinemann, 1939)

CHRONOLOGY

1870	Born on 3 January in Melbourne. Christened Ethel Florence Lindesay Richardson. Her father Dr Walter Richardson is conclusively converted to spiritualism by a successful experiment with automatic writing.
1871	Birth of her sister Lil (Ada Lillian Lindesay) who, unlike Ettie, is not christened, in keeping with her father's abandonment of religious orthodoxy.
1873	Family travels to London as a prelude to the parents' 'grand tour' of the Continent.
1874	Forced return to Melbourne through unexpected loss of revenue. Father returns to medical practice.
1875	Family moves to newly constructed home and practice in Hawthorn.
1876	Family moves in July to a country practice in Chiltern, Victoria. Summer 1876–77: clear signs of her father's cerebral deterioration and that his medical practice is close to collapse.
1877	Family moves to Queenscliff after fourteen months in Chiltern.
1878	Walter placed in medical care, first in Richmond and then in a mental asylum at Kew. Family moves to Koroit where his wife Mary takes up postal duties.
1879	Walter, in the final stages of general paralysis, is transferred to Koroit, where he dies five months later at the post office on 1 August, aged 53. Ettie develops severe facial twitches — an outward expression of the extreme disturbance which these events cause.

1880	Mary is appointed postmistress at Maldon through the political influence of family friend Henry Cuthbert. As a woman, however, she earns only £120; her male predecessor had received £220.
1883	Attends Presbyterian Ladies' College (PLC) as a boarder.
1884	Makes important academic progress and her musical talent is noted.
1886	Is strongly attracted to fellow boarder Constance (Connie) Cochran. Distinguishes herself as musical performer and composer.
1887	Family moves in January to Melbourne, where Mary heads the Richmond South post office until she resigns in May. End of Ettie's schooling at PLC.
1888	Teaches at a Toorak private school where she encounters the German Romantic heritage in Longfellow's *Hyperion: A Romance*. Sale of the Hawthorn house finances the family's voyage to England.
1889	Family moves to Leipzig. Start of specialised musical studies.
1890	Meets John George Robertson (born Glasgow, 18 January 1867), who is studying for his doctorate. Romance blossoms during their shared study of Wagnerian opera.
1891	Engaged to Robertson on 20 February.
1892	Concludes her musical studies at the end of the academic year (17 April), one year short of the minimum period for obtaining a formal musical qualification. Family returns to England and eventually settles near Cambridge. Robertson completes his PhD but is unable to find a university appointment in England.
1894	Begins work as essayist and translator. Family moves to London where Ettie sees the famous actress Eleonora Duse who serves, in part, as a model for Louise Dufrayer. Robertson, now in Scotland, works on scholarly articles and editions.

1895	Family moves to Munich, where Lil wishes to study the violin. Publishes 'Music Study in Leipzig', begins giving private English lessons. Marries Robertson in Dublin on 30 December.
1896	Heinemann publishes her translations of *Siren Voices (Niels Lyhne)* by Jens Peter Jacobsen and *The Fisher Lass* by Björnstjerne Björnson. Moves to Strasburg where Robertson is appointed a university lector in English. Mary dies of cancer in Munich on 26 November, aged 57.
1897	Commences serious work on *Maurice Guest.* Publishes 'Ibsen in translation' and 'A Danish Poet'. Extensive reading of Flaubert, Stendhal, Turgenev.
1898	Extensive reading of Nietzsche, Schopenhauer, Balzac. Is sent to the Riviera to recuperate from a serious attack of bronchitis.
1899	Death of a nearby child which will allegedly inspire 'The Life and death of Peterle Lüthy'. Rereads *Also sprach Zarathustra* and Flaubert.
1900	Her reading includes Hoffmann's *Die Brüder Seraphim,* containing 'Der Arthushof' and D'Annunzio's *Il Fuoco.* Lil marries eye-specialist Dr Otto Neustatter in Munich.
1901	Her reading includes Wedekind's *Erdgeist,* as well as *Die Geburt der Tragödie* and other works by Nietzsche.
1902	Lends works by Hoffmann and Wedekind to Lil and reads more works by Nietzsche. Robertson's *History of German Literature* published.
1903	Robertson appointed foundation Professor of German Literature at London University.
1904	Settles in Harrow. England becomes her permanent home. Occasional trips to the Continent. Leads an increasingly reclusive existence.
1907	Revisits Leipzig to verify details of *Maurice Guest.*
1908	*Maurice Guest* published.
1910	*The Getting of Wisdom* published. Moves to Regent's Park Road, London.

1911	Publication of 'Death' (a fictional response to her mother's death), later reprinted as 'Mary Christina'.
1912	Revisits Australia to gather material for *Australia Felix*. Enters into regular correspondence with Mary Kernot.
1917	*Australia Felix* published.
1919	Meets Olga Roncoroni (aged 26) at Lyme Regis.
1925	*The Way Home* published.
1927	Lil marries A. S. Neill and assists him with the experimental school Summerhill.
1928	Heinemann rejects the completed manuscript of *Ultima Thule*. It will be issued initially at Robertson's expense.
1929	*Ultima Thule* published, as well as 'The bath: an aquarelle' and 'Henry Handel Richardson', on the writing of *The Fortunes of Richard Mahony. Ultima Thule* will be awarded the Australian Literature Society's Gold Medal for 'the best Australian novel of 1929'.
1930	The three volumes published together as *The Fortunes of Richard Mahony*, as well as 'The story of Wagner and von Bülow — and the women behind their music'. Five-week boat cruise in the West Indies.
1931	Limited edition published of *Two Studies* (contents 'Mary Christina' and 'Life and death of Peterle Lüthy'), and 'The grown-up ball' or 'And women must weep'.
1932	Brief voyage to South Africa.
1933	Death of Robertson on 28 May, aged 66. Publication of 'The professor's experiment' and 'The wrong turning'.
1934	Moves to 'Green Ridges' in Sussex. *The End of a Childhood and Other Stories* published. A number of these stories appear separately, including 'Succedaneum' under the title 'Substance and shadow'.
1935	Awarded the King George V Jubilee Medal. Visited by Nettie Palmer.
1939	*The Young Cosima* published, and 'Sister Ann' written (published 1949). Begins work on a new novel which will never be completed. Final car and walking tour of Switzerland on the eve of World War II.

1940 'The Coat' published, as well as 'Some notes on my books'. Battle of Britain starts. 'Green Ridges' is suddenly in the front line. Suffers repeated illnesses and failing eyesight. Refuses to move to safety inland because of her attachment to the sea. Her home suffers bomb damage.

1941 Is adversely affected by food rationing. Sales of *The Young Cosima* affected by anti-German sentiment. *The Fortunes of Richard Mahony* is dramatised in the United States.

1942 Renewed coastal air-raids. First eight chapters of *Nick and Sanny* completed. Confined to bed for long periods.

1943 Though depressed by deteriorating health, living conditions, and the fact that all her books are now out of print, she works determinedly on the manuscript of *Myself When Young* (published 1948).

1944 Reads from the Proem to *The Way Home* for the BBC. The arrival of flying-bombs adds to the Sussex ordeal. Death of Lil, 30 April. Discovers that she is suffering from her mother's fatal disease, cancer of the colon.

1945 Metro-Goldwyn-Mayer offers to buy the film rights to *The Fortunes of Richard Mahony.* Greer Garson and Gregory Peck are to play the key roles.

1946 Her last 'full' letter is written to Mary Kernot at the end of January, and she has barely sufficient strength to sign the MGM contract a fortnight later. Dies 20 March, aged 76. She is cremated at Golders Green, and her ashes, together with those of Robertson, are scattered on the English Channel.

1 The Secret Self

Henry Handel Richardson was not only the author of one of Australia's finest novels, but also the creator of one of this country's most elusive public personae. Christened Ethel Florence Lindesay Richardson, and known to her family and friends as Ettie, she subsequently adopted the name of a maternal uncle as the foremost of a series of screens behind which she proceeded to establish herself as a major writer.

This act of revisionary self-imaging had many counterparts in her life. The embarrassing claret-red birthmark which ran from her shoulder down to her right hand was as carefully hidden from sight as childhood traumas and later suicidal impulses.[1] Similarly, the disappointment of her early musical ambitions was replaced by the projection of herself as a nascent wordsmith who, while working as a translator, recognised the true pleasure afforded by 'sit[ting] alone and unobserved, behind a shut door, and play[ing] with words and ponder[ing] phrases'.[2] Physically she put oceans between her past and present by moving permanently to Europe in 1888, much as her preferred writing environments were marked by a concerted withdrawal from daily existence behind soundproofed doors and rigid domestic routines. Though she freely drew on her life to fashion her major fiction, the debts are largely concealed behind an impersonal, even-handed narrative art, and would have provided only limited scope for biographical speculation were it not for her journals, letters and occasional writings. But these do exist, and they show, as Richardson confessed of *The Fortunes of Richard Mahony*, that 'the woof of fact and fiction is so intricately spun that, even for their author, the unravelling would now prove a difficult and lengthy task'.[3] Some of these connections, however, bear so directly on her fiction as to demand brief mention, while the significance of others, such as her abiding concern with issues as diverse as feminism, spiritualism and syphilis, has been too long underplayed.

Richardson's formative years were passed in a household undergoing tumultuous change, and later in a school which emphasised the need for young women to take responsibility for their own destiny. Though unaware of its causes at the time, Ettie, a noticing child like her later creations Laura and Cuffy, was acutely aware of her father's growing strangeness, as symptoms of tertiary syphilis began to leave their horrific marks on his once proud person. Something of the child's shock and shame is captured in her portrait of Cuffy's response to his father's growing dementia; as Dorothy Green notes, 'we are spared nothing except the usual fatuity of expression in these patients'.[4] Ettie's sense of humiliation and helplessness was intense, indeed indelible, to judge from its later fictional recasting, as was the learning experience it afforded. For her father's mental degeneration coincided with her family's increasing impoverishment. These changes led to the transformation of a Victorian patriarchal household into a domain where women worked, suffered and succeeded without the usual buffer afforded by male custodianship. In her mother's fall from gentility to the level of a toiling country postmistress, Ettie saw at first hand the need for female self-reliance, and for a gifted woman to pursue her own career even in the face of entrenched prejudice. Whatever else her subsequent years as a boarder at the Presbyterian Ladies' College in Melbourne brought her — and *The Getting of Wisdom* suggests that its legacy was definitely problematical — she found herself in a leading school dedicated to furthering female education and career possibilities. These goals, in turn, were part of a larger movement for women's rights and equality, which eventually produced legal reforms, the vote for women and public debate on issues ranging from diet to divorce, as well as the rise to local prominence of such feminist advocates as Catherine Helen Spence, Louisa Lawson and Rose Scott.

These youthful impressions were reinforced by her experience as a music student in Leipzig. Here, in a centre of European culture and supposedly enlightened thinking, which had recently been home to the likes of Richard Wagner, Friedrich Nietzsche and Franz Liszt, she saw the severe restrictions placed on female endeavours. Compositions by women had little chance of being performed, and dynamic creative spirits among her sex could at best aspire to be Cosima-like handmaidens to male genius. The sphere of women, according to German orthodoxy, was confined to feeling, service and motherhood, or as one of her least lovable characters, Dove, put it: 'A woman's way of looking at these things is, thank God, humaner than ours. But it's a man's duty not to let his feelings run away with him' (*MG* 483). Also she encountered a wave of avant-garde misogyny which variously depicted women as destroying *femmes fatales*, or as a biologically impoverished and secondary sex — a view which later achieved special prominence through the inflammatory writings of Otto Weininger and the early essays of Sigmund Freud.

Richardson, to judge from her later fiction, found these stereotypes demeaning and unacceptable. In 1892 she left Leipzig, one year short of the minimum four years required to complete a diploma, but not before she had met John George Robertson, whose influence was destined to eclipse that of her musical mentors. Robertson, a Science–Arts graduate from Glasgow, had come to the Continent to pursue a passion for German letters which would eventually carry him to the chair of German literature at London University. A man of liberal views and great erudition, he fostered Ettie's literary education and creative unfolding. He also provided the emotional anchor which had been missing from her life, fulfilling a variety of roles during their thirty-seven-year marriage which she summed up after his death: 'In him I lose husband, father, brother rolled in one. He was everything to me.'[5] Their union affords a neat emblem of key influences on her fiction — Continental culture and personal experience — and of the ideal of companionate marriage projected by feminist reformers at the turn of the century.

Like George Eliot, her first sustained literary performance was as a translator, in Richardson's case of Scandinavian fiction by Jens Peter Jacobsen and Björnstjerne Björnson. This work helped her to move from music to literature as her primary creative medium,[6] and afforded a firm grounding in that highly crafted naturalism, coupled with psychological penetration, which is a hallmark of Flaubert and his successors. Less often remarked is the importance of Jacobsen to Richardson as an acute depicter of female predicaments. She singles out his *Fru Marie Grubbe* as providing not only an example of what

Goethe called a 'problematical nature', but more specifically a psychological study of a woman who 'spends her life in a vain search after an ideal'.[7] Similarly *Niels Lyhne*, the novel she translated, may be of 'unsurpassable worth' for 'the picture it gives of the growth and development of a poetic, introspective nature', but this is then rephrased as a '"sentimental education" ... unfolded [through] ... an analysis of the temporary relations in which he stands to various women'.[8] Among them is Niels' mother Batholine who, Richardson-like, feels drawn to poetry rather than to diurnal getting-and-spending, and asks: 'how do I know what I am?'[9] Jacobsen's ensuing analysis is at once subtle and devastating, and would have been of special interest to a novice writer in anxious quest of her own identity and calling:

> Strictly speaking, there was really nothing in this but the slightly morbid desire to become conscious of herself, the endeavour to realise herself, that so often awakens in a young girl of more than ordinary talent, but the misfortune was that there was not a single superior nature in her whole circle of acquaintances by which she might have measured her own gifts; there was not even a congenial nature, and therefore she began to consider herself something extraordinary and exceptional, a sort of tropical plant which had shot up under an unfriendly sky and could only make a pitiful attempt to unfold its leaves, whereas in a warmer clime, beneath a brighter sun, it would have put forth slender stems, crowned with a rich and radiant show of flowers. That, she thought, was her real nature; that was what the proper surroundings would have made her; and she dreamed a thousand dreams of those sunny places and was consumed with longing for her true, rich self, forgetting what it is so easy to forget, that even the fairest dreams, even the deepest longings, add not a single inch to the stature of the human soul.[10]

Ettie, fresh from her setback in Leipzig, could hardly not have been struck by the personal application of such a passage. Was she really set apart by special talents? Or was her early high self-estimation the product of a colonial society that afforded little against which she could adequately measure her true worth? Launching herself in the world of publishing was one way of finding out, while Richardson would not have been blind to the condescending paternalism implicit in Jacobsen's description of Batholine; he recounts ironically how 'the poets said distinctly that *this* [creative activity] was life, and that sewing and knitting, doing housework and paying stupid visits was not life at all'.[11] Richardson, with time, would reject neither calling as viable alternatives for her sex, and in Mary Mahony raise an enduring memorial to these unsung contributions. She herself, however, with Robertson's acquiescence, turned her back on conventional female roles. Not only did she proselytise for *A Room of One's Own*,[12] but during her marriage she insisted on having her own personal sphere, and fulfilled Batholine's dream by putting her creative calling far above domestic duties.

> By 9 a.m. she was dressed, and went down to the kitchen to arrange meals for the day. Her study had been cleaned while she breakfasted; the flowers arranged; her trayful of pencils sharpened by her husband and placed on the writing-table. By 9.30 she had shut her study door (and the specially made sound-proof door outside it); and heaven help anyone who intruded or disturbed her before 12.30 or 1 p.m.[13]

The old notion of her lack of interest in the women's movement, buttressed by her secluded existence and by a limited reading of her fiction, has recently given way to awareness of her intense engagement with women's issues: 'she was a radical feminist, an active supporter of the suffragettes, and an admirer of Olive Schreiner'.[14] Her sister Lilian, with whom Ettie exchanged ideas and books, was a suffragette jailed for her part in civil disturbances. Ettie was sufficiently engaged emotionally and intellectually in these doings to have her work disrupted during 1911–12, and to envisage postponing her fact-finding return to Australia. Similarly, her letters to close correspondents leave no doubt as to where her sympathies lay. With Mary Kernot she could openly deride patriarchal nonsense about what constituted appropriate female knowledge and literary themes, or dilate on the need for women's suffrage or protest strikes, to the extent that her Australian friend, who confessed to 'now & then cast[ing] a bomb into the usual conversation', found that Ettie's remarks had a 'yeasty effect' even on her.[15] The same spirit which propelled Richardson at school to set up a Society for Suppressing Idiots is discernible in her fictional critiques of unthinking female minds. In *The Getting of Wisdom* Inez is attacked for having 'a real woman's brain: vague, slippery, inexact, interested only in the personal aspect of a thing. ... and, worst of all, you've no curiosity — about anything that really matters' (*GW* 89); in *Maurice*

Guest Richardson dramatises these female failings, and descants scathingly on the kinds of fiction which cater to them:

> Mrs. Cayhill was a handsome woman, who led a comfortable, vegetable existence, and found it a task to rise from the plump sofa-cushion. Her pleasant features were slack, and in those moments of life which called for a sudden decision, they wore the helpless bewilderment of a woman who has never been required to think for herself. Her grasp on practical matters was rendered the more lax, too, by her being an immoderate reader, who fed on novels from morning till night, and slept with a page turned down beside her bed. ... All novels were fish to Mrs. Cayhill's net; she lived in a world of intrigue and excitement, and, seated in her easy-chair by the sitting-room window, was generally as remote from her family as though she were in Timbuctoo. (*MG* 72–3)

Non-compliant in her art and life, Richardson pursued a career which recalls those of other late nineteenth-century women writers who had to struggle against ingrained conceptions of literary authority as a male prerogative, and of male experience as normative. In adopting a pen-name she consciously put herself beyond the normal strictures aimed at her sex and asserted an independent identity: 'Richardson was the name I was born with — and perhaps I place an almost oriental valuation on a personal name; any way, why should a woman lose her name on marriage? As for Henry, well, *Maurice Guest* appeared at a time of feminist agitation, and I wanted the book to be a test. No one, positively no reviewer, spotted it as "just a woman's work".'[16] The renaming was an act of empowerment and a licence to transgress. It afforded her privacy and security, as did her later domestic arrangements, as well as an imaginative freedom expressed later in the bold working motto of 'Nichts vertuschen, nichts verzerren' ('Cover up nothing, distort nothing').[17] Writing may, to paraphrase the conclusion of *The Getting of Wisdom*, provide a realm where even misfits or the alienated are at home, where the world dances to one's tune and where other standards apply. But in Ettie's view it also demanded an intensity of artistic commitment and a striving after fundamental truths which placed her, or a recognised 'mental aristocrat' like Jacobsen,[18] at odds with the vacuous romances traditionally assigned to womankind.

Richardson's own peculiar form of remoteness from daily concerns, unlike Mrs Cayhill's, was spiritualism, although even this had politicised ramifications. While its chief appeal lay undoubtedly in 'proofs' of the continuance of individual existences after death and of their accessibility to the living, spiritualism, from its outset, was a movement which granted women unusual privileges. Not only were its founders the American sisters Kate and Margaret Fox, but through it women achieved special prominence as mediums, and as public speakers or performers they could draw large audiences. Within the seance itself, normal gender restrictions were often relaxed, as notions of propriety and womanliness fell victim to the paranormal. Seen positively, at its peak in the late nineteenth century 'spiritualism validated the female authoritative voice and permitted women an active professional and spiritual role largely denied them elsewhere'.[19] Its negative aspects were that this empowerment depended on such female stereotypes as passivity and mutable identity, and that the ascendancy women gained from trafficking with the paranormal usually stopped at the doorway to the seance. Richardson would have been fascinated by the questions spiritualism raised concerning personal identity, authority and the supernatural. She was introduced to it through her father's involvement in spiritualist activities in Victoria, and by his contributions to its monthly magazine, the *Harbinger of Light*. Later she 'belonged to three psychic research societies',[20] and attested to first-hand experience of a range of 'psychic' phenomena, from spirits of the departed to *Poltergeister*, whose knockings and antics entertained the Robertson family circle and disconcerted occasional guests.[21]

Ettie's putatively 'life-long adherence to Spiritualism' shaped crucial chapters of her fiction and of her private affairs.[22] Creatively, this preoccupation assumes significant but carefully qualified forms. In 'The Coat' the alleged coexistence of diverse types of existence and consciousness enables Richardson to evoke the experience of a fatally injured woman crossing spiritual thresholds. *The Fortunes of Richard Mahony* ends affirmatively by asserting life's continuity, not its definitive eclipse. More personally, her letters from the 1930s chart the transcendence of a profound despondency linked with the imminent or actual loss of her husband: 'After this he dropped asleep and slept on. I lay for a couple of hours, at least, and cried and despaired. Tried to think *what* my life would be without him — him for whom I write my books alone, the sight of whose dear face has always filled every want I have had.'[23] Yet spiritualist faith would enable her to contact him through a medium, and to achieve a calm denied her occasionally during his lifetime by his unscheduled movements, because of her assurance that death conducted the spirit to a permanent, secure and yet contiguous realm: 'Odd to think that I shall never need to be troubled about his whereabouts again. Death has *had* him; it is over; he is safe now for ever. My heart can be at rest in his eternal absence.'[24]

Hence, too, the woman who for years had sought uninterrupted working conditions could withstand with apparent composure the daily dangers of living on the south coast of England during the height of the Battle of Britain. 'If I stop a bomb, well, I do, & that's all about it. I've lived my life & done my main work, & in a way shall not be sorry to leave this world for the next, where carnage & slaughter are unknown.'[25] Spiritualism gave her assurance in the face of personal loss and impending demise, and allowed her to assert confidently on 29 April 1941: 'the death of the body doesn't mean as much to me as it does to others; for I look on death not as an ending but as a new beginning; & one offering more & better chances than this earthly life'.[26]

One 'ghost' that Richardson did not wish to face when she attended seances was the fear of syphilis, though confront it she did at important stages of her life. The first shocking contact came with the degenerative death of her father, which cast a deep shadow over her early years in Australia. Nor was she able to dispel it by moving to the Continent, for there she found that syphilis had assumed in the public consciousness the dimensions of the current AIDS epidemic. Known as 'the great imitator' because of the variety of symptoms it could assume, the spectre of syphilis stalked European streets, such as those of pre-war Vienna where, as 'Stefan Zweig recalled, every sixth house had a sign advertising a specialist in venereal disease, and all his friends feared infection'.[27] Similarly, in 1913 Christabel Pankhurst was not simply underscoring the consequences of sexual double standards when she asserted that seventy-five to eighty per cent of Englishmen were infected with gonorrhoea, and a frightening number with syphilis.[28] She was articulating the dread of generations, at a time when knowledge about the spread and cure of syphilis was still limited. In particular, rumour about its transmission to the innocent was rampant, and even reliable modern data are disquieting: namely that the presence of the disease in a pregnant woman leads to a fourfold increase in the possibility of a stillbirth, double the likelihood of infant mortality, and the probability that twenty per cent of surviving offspring will have congenital syphilis. Some of these dangers were known to Richardson, as was the fact that 'my mother had several miscarriages before I was born'.[29] These widespread concerns were graphically focused for her, as for her contemporaries, by Henrik Ibsen's dramatisation of sexual sin and hypocrisy in *Ghosts*. The title refers at once to our parental inheritance and to those outmoded conventions which stifle the living. Osvald, a promising young artist, is condemned to insanity by the debauchery of his father, being 'vermoulu' or 'worm-eaten' by syphilis from birth. His mother, Mrs Alving, with the aid of the local clergyman, attempts to blot out her husband's misdemeanours by building an orphanage to his memory — only to see it burn down. Ettie, eschewing both parenthood and the temptation to sanitise the past,[30] preferred to set a far different monument to her parents in her major novel, which locates in their sufferings and failings a measure of the true depth and quality of their union.

Exactly when Richardson grasped the reasons behind her father's unseemly demise is uncertain,[31] but questions related to sexual impropriety, and syphilis in particular, constantly engaged her creative faculties. In *Maurice Guest* we hear of '*Ghosts*, which was being read by a bold, advanced few', in conjunction with an interest in 'continental methods of regulating vice' (*MG* 45); *The Fortunes of Richard Mahony* details the ravages of tertiary syphilis, and covertly its place in her life. It has been documented that 'she was deep in medical books before 1914',[32] and that she was well versed in the findings of such standard texts as W. J. Mickle's *On General Paralysis of the Insane* (1886). Less obviously, this preoccupation emerges arguably in a refracted form in her shorter fiction. The early death of Peterle Lüthy, for example, which is attributed to infant cholera, raises the spectre of maternally transmitted syphilis — a hypothesis supported as much by his mother's promiscuity as by his final wizened form: a hallmark of the innocent syphilitic which scarified the Victorian imagination. 'The Professor's Experiment', although offering a credible explanation for its own unfolding action, recalls more familiar narratives where the male's experiment is sexual, morally forbidden, and risks dangerous infection, as the diverse careers of Friedrich Nietzsche and Walter Richardson testify. Similarly, it recasts the almost clichéd female responses of shocked outrage and disbelief at the unexpected revelation in intricate ways, calling to mind a recent observation on 'the attempts of Richardson's psychoanalytic fiction to bury alive the entities it represses'.[33] Only Mahony, who is well equipped by his medical training to diagnose the symptoms of paresis, or general paralysis of the insane, the most dreaded tertiary manifestation of syphilis, comes close to articulating this secret fear. Yet even he seeks to avoid the ultimate act of naming, 'though, with a part of his mind, a watchful part, a part that it was impossible to deceive, he *knew* what it was' (*RM* 828).

Unlike her fictional alter ego, Richardson found an outlet for her preoccupations and dreads in creative activity. Often she presented writing as an escape which made life tolerable. More precisely, it was also a way of exorcising, or at least controlling, deeply felt concerns. For she was, as Olga Roncoroni reported of her friend's unorthodox beliefs, a person who 'held that one made one's own hell: a purely mental one'.[34] Nietzsche, one of her favourite authors, said much the same thing in the section headed 'The Path of the Creator' in *Thus Spoke Zarathustra*:

> But the worst enemy whom you can meet will always be yourself; you lie in wait for yourself in caves and forests.
>
> Solitary one, you are on the path to yourself! Your path leads past you yourself, and past your seven devils![35]

Typically, Richardson could conceive of this creative process in spiritualist terms: 'Not only to fight through experiences but to distil from them the essence — not moral, or instructive, or artistic, but spiritual — that will best serve that sly interloper, the soul.'[36] But that it also involved confronting personal devils emerges from retrospective comments on her first novel: '"Here in a distant place I hold my tongue, / Who once said all my say, when I was young!"' or it 'was written in my youth — at a time of life when one is usually rather hot & bitter'.[37] These private impulses would be further mastered with what Mary Kernot dubbed her 'old god-like habit': 'You have brought these people out of dimness & made them live intensely in their passions & frailties & yet you leave me in perplexity as to the rights & wrongs of every one.'[38] To penetrate beneath this detached narrative art, worthy of a Flaubert, is a major aim of this study, because she, no less than the Jacobsen described in her essay, hid her 'sensitiveness and rich inner life under a veil of reserve which was rarely raised, and the quiet irony, now pungent, now gently humorous, that … was only another form of self defence'.[39] In particular, I want to raise the veil on neglected aspects of the Australian's lifelong engagement with German culture, which proved to be a source of inspiration as well as of admonitory examples, and to demonstrate the ways in which the shy, socially inept author, once safely immured within her writing sanctum, set about confronting her 'seven devils' and boldly reshaping literary traditions, as she endeavoured to come to terms with her personal legacy and to rethink gender conventions.

2 Decentring the *Künstler-roman*: *Maurice Guest*

From the outset *Maurice Guest* was a work with an agenda, but that agenda changed considerably during its long period of gestation and composition. Richardson began her manuscript falteringly, unsure of herself and the full scope of her undertaking. So far she was known as a translator and essayist. Her dreams of a musical career had been dispelled, and she was married to a man whose life was devoted to literature, and whose research made heavy demands on his time. She needed an occupation, and a means to test the belief, inculcated in girlhood, that a special destiny awaited her. Authorship became her goal, and a pencilled remark in the margin of her own copy of *Maurice Guest* at the end of the first three pages reads: 'Up to about here given to Nub for a first reading one day in Jan 1897. A never-to-be-forgotten day. I went & walked in the snow while he read.'[1] The response was encouraging. Work proceeded, together with a comprehensive reading program of recent European authors which was duly recorded in her diaries. Subsequent marginaliae in *Maurice Guest* indicate a slow process of thematic focusing. 'The remainder of this [third] chapter was written later on when I knew what I wanted to put into it',[2] or two pages into chapter four: 'There was a considerable time gap here; then suddenly one day in the Twinger I got these pages.'[3] By the time the work appeared in 1908 Richardson had found a vocation as well as her major themes, and had produced a book which subverted one of the most venerable traditions of the novel — that of the *Bildungsroman* or novel of education.

The opening pages given to 'Nub' for vetting bear the hallmarks of a typical *Bildungsroman*. The protagonist is introduced as a young man aspiring to musical acclaim, and standing before a resonant symbol of his grail: the Gewandhaus concert hall in Leipzig. Romantic longing is conjured up as Maurice's gaze seeks in vain for mountain vistas 'blue with the unapproachable blue of distance' (*MG* 5). The world lies in imagination at his feet, but all will depend on this crucial phase of individual formation upon which he is about to embark. A reader familiar with any of the classical texts of the genre, such as *Tom Jones* or *Wilhelm Meister*, would expect Maurice to remain the principal concern, and for him to undergo a series of encounters which give definite shape to his character and form him for an active life in the world. Self-knowledge and social integration will normally be won with time, as the hero overcomes the dictates of blind nature, and moves from the realm of empty or fabulous dreams to assume familial and/or vocational duties near at hand. The same holds broadly true for the *Künstlerroman* (artist-novel), a specialised form of the *Bildungsroman* concerned specifically with the life and formative influences of an artist, in works such as James Joyce's *Portrait of the Artist as a Young Man*, Patrick White's *The Vivisector* and Richardson's *Maurice Guest* and *The Getting of Wisdom*. *Maurice Guest*, however, disappoints the usual expectations raised by the genre. For one thing, Maurice never develops into a fully fledged artist figure, nor does he achieve maturity, inner harmony or success. More importantly, he is often eclipsed as the main focal point of psychological interest by female protagonists, as gender issues gradually challenge the novel's ostensible focus on artistic concerns.

Richardson, as has been often documented, was thoroughly versed in nineteenth-century fiction and in the traditions of the *Bildungsroman* and *Künstlerroman*. Her husband, J. G. Robertson, in his well-known essay on 'The Art of Henry Handel Richardson', draws attention to the abiding influence of the naturalist fiction of France, Russia and Scandinavia. *Maurice Guest* itself he terms a 'kind of mosaic of influences', and names writers such as Flaubert, Balzac, Turgenev, Dostoevsky and D'Annunzio.[4] This list is supported by Richardson's diary entries on her reading at the turn of the century, and could be extended further in the sphere of German letters, given her mastery of the language and her husband's expertise in this field. She was, for instance, certainly familiar with such major German novels of education as Goethe's *Wilhelm Meister* and Novalis's *Heinrich von Ofterdingen*. Their example provides a silent backdrop to *Maurice*

Guest, and a yardstick against which to measure Richardson's use of the genre. To focus only on some obvious parallels, the concept of *Wanderjahre*, or the years of roving apprenticeship preceding mastery, which is used to describe the early life of Maurice's father and re-echoed in his son's journey from Glasgow to Leipzig, is central to Goethe's prototypal novel. There the hero, much like Maurice, follows an artistic calling — in Wilhelm's case the theatre. Neither protagonist is fulfilled by this endeavour, but Maurice's eventual turning from it is equated with a rejection of bourgeois values, whereas for Wilhelm this is a vital stage in his maturation and later return to responsible action in the wider community. Novalis is also an important precursor, and Maurice's enigmatic friend Krafft reports having immersed himself in the Romantic's works while convalescing from illness. So, too, had Richardson, as is evident from the role assumed by Maurice's vision of Louise. In *Heinrich von Ofterdingen* the male lead dreams of, and feels impelled to pursue, a beautiful blue flower, which is subsequently identified with his female soul-mate. Similarly Maurice, afflicted by a germinating passion, mentally links Louise with a rose seen in her room, until 'in the troubled image that at last crowned his patience, her eyes looked out, like jewels, from a setting of golden petals' (*MG* 35). For Heinrich, the consequence of this vision is a fruitful pilgrimage which leads him 'immer nach Hause' — 'always home' in the sense of integration and self-realisation. Also Goethe's Wilhelm learns the mistake of seeking fulfilment far from home, or in the words of his mentor Jarno: 'Hier oder nirgend ist Amerika!' ('Here or nowhere is America!').[5] For Maurice, however, pursuit of the fabulous blue horizon or flower leads to a severance from his origins, and signals a shift from personal dominion and self-mastery towards eventually destructive impulses.

Richardson was doing nothing new in making her eponymous hero fail as an artist — her innovations lay elsewhere. As Robertson noted, the ostensible story-line of 'insufficient ability for the chosen calling' was 'well-worn' and seemed arguably 'too trite to provide a foundation for still another variation'. Her response, he concludes, was to graft onto it 'a love-story of such elemental force that the first conception of the "stickit musician" has been dwarfed almost into insignificance'.[6] Unwittingly, Robertson thereby established the broad outline of future debate on this work. Was Richardson concerned primarily with the constituents of true genius following a Nietzschean model, as A. D. Hope has argued?[7] Or is the work's interest first and foremost in the tragic love entanglement of Maurice and Louise, as Dorothy Green has ably countered?[8] Both, it seems to me, are central preoccupations; however, the novel's interest for modern readers lies more probably in its penetrating studies of different female types, and in its much underrated contribution to the 'Frauenproblem', or the question of women's place and role, which was as much a burning issue then as it is today.

Maurice Guest contains a fascinating gallery of female figures who, by and large, are much better realised than their male counterparts. These women range across ages, nations and sexual predilections. Most memorable perhaps are the romance-devouring American dowager Mrs Cayhill, her two temperamentally opposed daughters Ephie and Johanna, the pragmatic Madeleine, and her contrary in the emotion-driven Louise. In contrast, even major masculine protagonists like Krafft and Schilsky appear primarily as spokespersons for, or representatives of, key concepts, while Richardson rightly spoke of 'that Simple Simon Maurice Guest'.[9] His is a singularly unremarkable personality, and he is constantly cast as the outsider, observer and narrative link between dramatic scenes which highlight specifically female dilemmas. That Richardson had in mind a typology of her sex is also suggested by a brief working-note preserved by Olga Roncoroni:

> The sexual woman = Louise
> The instinctive = Madeleine. No, the brave strong motherly woman.
> Now I ought to do the intellectual.[10]

Johanna Cayhill was presumably the result although, as the mid-sentence reappraisal of Madeleine suggests, these categories were fluid or subject to revision. The distinction between the male and female portrayals can be further underlined if we imagine similar notations for the male leads. They might read, if we concentrate on the central focus of each male character:

> Schilsky = artistic genius
> Krafft = gifted and anarchic
> Dove = talent pragmatically applied
> Maurice = Simple Simon, of limited imaginative capacity in human and artistic dealings.

As these lists show, to argue that Richardson's prime concern is with the nature of genius is to highlight one aspect of the work, a risk shared by the contrary emphasis on love. Instead, a common basis is to be found in the notion of vocation, with male characters, in keeping with their traditional identification with the intellectual sphere, being largely responsible for direct conceptual input into the text, while female characters afford practical examples of the life-choice awaiting their sex, as well as dramatisations of contemporary stereotypes and theories.

This interest in the woman question is hardly surprising in view of the writer's upbringing, and especially of the intellectual debate which she encountered in Europe. The fight for women's emancipation was well advanced in Australia by the 1880s, as was discussion about the relative importance of socialisation over physiological factors in shaping womankind. Nevertheless, there was little in the anglophone world to compare with the speculative ferment emanating from Vienna and avidly followed in Leipzig, Munich and Strasburg, where Richardson spent eleven decisive years. This enlarged intellectual heritage is confirmed by her own testimony and by allusions in her subsequent works. An April entry from her 1898 diary, for instance, records having studied Arthur Schopenhauer's *Parerga und Paralipomena*, which contains the notoriously misogynist chapter 'Über die Weiber' ('About Women'). Equally topical is her characterisation of Schilsky, the undisputed musical genius of *Maurice Guest.* Not only is his outward appearance based on that of Richard Strauss, but his intellectual lodestars are indicated by his original compositions entitled *Also sprach Zarathustra* and *Über die letzten Dinge.* The Nietzschean source of the first has long been recognised, but the debt of the latter to the Viennese philosopher Otto Weininger has been forgotten, and with it vital clues to Richardson's attitude towards Schilsky and to her presentation of gender relations.

Today Otto Weininger (1880–1903) is chiefly remembered for outmoded sexist and racist theories. In the first decade of the century, however, his reputation stood higher. Of Jewish extraction, he converted to Protestantism at the end of his university studies and quickly made a name for himself as a polemicist and antifeminist. This was assured in 1903 by the publication of a 600–page treatise entitled *Geschlecht und Charakter* (*Sex and Character*). Its controversial matter created a sensation, as did his suicide little more than three months after its appearance. Like Maurice Guest, Weininger became convinced of the impossibility of life and sexual relations, and shot himself through the breast. Also his name had been linked with Sigmund Freud's and a plagiarism scandal. One of Freud's medical collaborators, Wilhelm Fliess of Berlin, had imparted key discoveries on bisexuality to the Viennese savant in correspondence, only to see them reduplicated in writings by Weininger and another young Viennese, Hermann Swoboda. Freud was apparently the unthinking intermediary of these theories. An indignant Fliess contributed to the currency of Weininger's name, as did the influential advocacy of his ideas by such intellectual tonesetters as Karl Kraus. Also the anti-Semitism of Weininger's *chef-d'oeuvre* struck a contemporary chord and, given his parentage, provided an unwitting demonstration of his own adage: 'We only hate what we resemble.'[11] Nevertheless, his name remained primarily associated with gender issues. In the words of one authority on the period, 'some saw in *Sex and Character* an almost pornographic work, for others however it represented the best compilation on the psychology of the sexes'.[12] With such a reputation, the work remained long in vogue, and was reissued almost yearly until its proscription by Fascist authorities in the 1930s as the work of a renegade Jew.

Über die letzten Dinge (*About the Last Things*) brought together posthumously Weininger's unpublished essays and aphorisms, and dealt with such founding figures of modernism as Ibsen and Wagner, who are also prominent in the intellectual milieu of *Maurice Guest.* Metaphysically, the scope of Weininger's collection is immense. It touches on cosmic, aesthetic and timeless issues, often in terms of irreducible dualities:

> Why do existence [das Etwas] and nothingness always strive against one another? Why was humanity born, why is man drawn to woman? The problem of love, as we see here, is the problem of the world, the problem of life — fathomless and for ever irresolvable — the impulse to form matter, the impulse of the timeless towards time, of the spaceless towards space. We encounter this problem everywhere: it is the relationship of freedom to necessity. The dualism of the world is incomprehensible: the motive for original sin a puzzle: the reason and sense and purpose of the fall from timeless being, from eternal life into non-being, into the life of the senses, into earthly temporality; the fall of those free from guilt into guilt.[13]

Such rambling speculation leaves the ultimate questions unanswered, but is clearer on one personally pressing issue: 'man lives until he is subsumed by the absolute or by nothingness. He freely defines his future life: he chooses God or nothingness. He destroys himself or creates himself for eternal life.'[14] Weininger seems to have chosen nothingness, whereas Schilsky is apparently striving towards a dubious musical immortality in the final scene of *Maurice Guest.* There the composer's return to Leipzig is associated with 'his new symphonic poem, *Über die letzten Dinge*, [which] had drawn down on his head that mixture of extravagant laudation and abusive derision, which constitutes fame', and with 'talking volubly to a Jewish-looking stranger in a fur-lined coat' (*MG* 561). The public response to both Schilsky's composition and his Jewish companion evokes Weininger and his ideas as surely as does a selfless, subservient Louise, who 'had no attention for anyone but her husband' (*MG* 562).

Of special relevance to *Maurice Guest* is Weininger's blatantly misogynist standpoint. Not only was he strongly opposed to any increase in women's sphere of influence, but in *Sex and Character* he set out systematically to explode what he saw as the unmarked myths by means of which females were able to exercise unwarranted sway. Below is a summary of some of his reiterated and typically denigratory views. The lowest man he adjudges superior to the highest type of woman, and this inferior sex is seen as being without individual identity, without soul, and reducible to a primary sexual drive: her overwhelming but cunningly dissembled desire for copulation. This also explains the immense efforts of women to ensure the coupling of their daughters and sisters with men, their disdain for spinsters, and their inherent inferiority to man who 'is sexual and something more besides' ('und noch etwas darüber').[15] Given her total identification with sexuality, the female of the species is without original consciousness, without desire for immortality, and entirely excluded from genius. Even the abiding stereotype, in Alexander Pope's words, of woman as 'at best a contradiction still' can now be categorically dismissed:

> *Woman as the sphinx! A worse stupidity can scarcely be uttered, or a worse swindle perpetrated. Man is endlessly more puzzling, incomparably more complicated.* You only need to go out into the street where you'll rarely encounter a woman's face whose expression doesn't soon become clear to

> you. Women's range of feelings and moods is infinitely impoverished [unendlich arm]. Whereas many men's faces provide matter for long and difficult reflection.[16]

This misogyny, coupled with his early death, made Weininger's work a much discussed modern classic in the decade preceding the Great War, and lent him almost hagiographic status in certain quarters, as August Strindberg's tribute of 1903 demonstrates: 'He dared to speak the known secret, to reveal the essence and nature of woman in his masculine book *Sex and Character*, and it cost him his life.'[17]

Finally, it should be noted that Weininger's misogyny formed part of a continuing local tradition, according to which, as a visiting American journalist in *Maurice Guest* is quick to note, 'the ordinary German woman was little more than a means to an end, the end being the man-child' (*MG* 144). During the nineteenth century successive German governments fostered the bourgeois family model, as well as women's procreative role, and anticipated the latter's elevation into a cornerstone of national ideology under the Hitler regime. These socio-political decisions received influential support from diverse sources, including normally radical philosophers. According to Schopenhauer, for instance, women occupied a middle stage between children and men.[18] Without large intellectual and physical capacities, they are inferior in reasoning and action, leading to a host of negative characteristics, such as a lack of honesty, fairness, conscientiousness, faithfulness and thankfulness. Given the sex's addiction to lies, cunning and dissembling, he asks pointedly whether women should even be admitted to oath-taking in court, and suggests banning them from theatres, where they otherwise disturb performances with their constant chatter. The sole occupation granted woman by Schopenhauer is to catch a man, her naturally ordained role is to propagate the species, and her social place is defined by subordination and obedience. Similar views recur in the works of subsequent German thinkers of the stature of Nietzsche, and these are occasionally cited by Weininger, as when his crude assertion of 'the ugliness of female genitals and the lack of beauty [Unschönheit] of her living body' is buttressed by a passage from Schopenhauer's 'Über die Weiber': 'That the small-grown, narrow-shouldered, wide-hipped, short-legged sex could be called the beautiful sex is explicable only in terms of male intellect overmastered by sexual desire [vom Geschlechtstrieb umnebelt] — and to this impulse is attributable her entire beauty.'[19] The possibility that such gender-related issues might assume an entirely different aspect if viewed from a female standpoint never trammels the prose of either Weininger or Schopenhauer, but we may be sure that it was a constant preoccupation for Richardson, and that it contributed to the approval with which she cited 'Goethe who said of his own people that, while valuable as individuals, as a nation they were hopeless'.[20]

Schilsky's final association with Weininger is, then, extremely telling. Although to a reader of Strindberg's predilections it could affirm the composer's heroic stature, viewed in terms of Schilsky's overall characterisation it provides climactic confirmation of his coarse and unchanged misogyny. For not only is he ruthless and self-centred in his dealings with women, but, in accordance with the masculinist premises of contemporary German thought, he views the opposite sex as unalterably inferior and, when liquor loosens his tongue, casts it as the timeless scapegoat of male failings: 'By Hell, I wish a plague would sweep every woman off the earth! ... Damn them all! — old and young — I say. If it weren't for them, a man could lead a quiet life' (*MG* 194). Similarly, from the vantage-point afforded by assumed male superiority he can echo Weininger in asserting: 'A woman has no gratitude ... It is a weak, childish sex — with no inkling of higher things' (*MG* 196). Nor is this local genius alone in his ingrained misogyny. It re-emerges in Maurice Guest during his later crises, and it is given definitive expression by Krafft:

> 'Believe me, women are all alike; they are made to be trodden on. Ill-usage brings out their good points — just as kneading makes dough light. Let them alone, or pamper them, and they spread like a weed, and choke you' — and he quoted a saying about going to women and not forgetting the whip, at which Maurice stood aghast. (*MG* 165)

The aphorism which Krafft quotes, and which is still current in modern German, derives from *Thus Spoke Zarathustra.* In the section headed 'Of old and young women' Nietzsche writes: '"Give me, woman, your small truth!" I said. And thus spoke the old woman: "Are you going off to women? Don't forget [to take] the whip!"'[21] Maurice's shocked reaction at this early stage of the novel condemns a patriarchal society which treats women as mindless breeders, and by extension the notorious womaniser Schilsky, whose claims to genius are identified closely with such well-known sources of misogynist thought as Weininger and Nietzsche.

In striking contrast to this generic, dismissive and often defamatory treatment of womankind, Richardson analyses the forces shaping individual women and challenges rigidly gender-based attitudes. Typically she conveys her viewpoint through cumulative dramatisations rather than direct statement. Thus the condescending truism that 'it was an ancient privilege of the ladies never to be obliged to know their own minds' (*MG* 227), uttered as an inane compliment to Ephie by a minor admirer, is not immediately rebutted — but is categorically disproved by the life-choices which confront every major female protagonist in the novel. Repeatedly, too, behavioural models shift unsettlingly to suggest the interchangeability, ambivalence or instability of gender categorisations, as in the initial encounter between Maurice and Madeleine. Their looks meet, and 'he was aware of a peculiarly straight and penetrating gaze. It ended by disconcerting him' (*MG* 8). Glancing away, Maurice completes a feminine response pattern by finishing in a nervous flutter, and is saved from embarrassment only by Madeleine's intervention. Nor, as Krafft illustrates, are sexual proclivities more assured than conventional roles of dominance and subordination. Though capable of preaching the Nietzschean doctrine of the *Übermensch* and of playing the male boon-companion, his latent bisexuality can call forth responses normally reserved for the opposite sex, as when Maurice, standing shoulder to shoulder with him on a bridge, 'did not [understand] how he could ever have taken anything this frail creature did, amiss. At the moment, there was a clinging helplessness about Krafft, which instinctively roused his manlier feelings' (*MG* 162). Successive scenes ruthlessly shake treasured notions of male upstandingness, female innocence and gender propriety, while subversive individual portraits show that there is far more to being a woman than stock physical markers indicate.

The theme of *Bildung*, or individual formation, is specifically related to the actualities of female experience through the complementary characterisation of the Cayhill sisters. When we meet them, the final finishing touches are to be placed on Ephie in Leipzig, while Johanna is evidently finished in the darker sense of having rendered herself ineligible for marriage by her age and intellectual aspirations. Ephie is highly admired by those who form her inner circle for her childlike aura of innocence. Johanna will happily sacrifice herself to preserve it (*MG* 81), and Maurice subscribes so completely to this misapprehension that it temporarily blinds him to Ephie's dangerous passion for Schilsky. Ephie is in many respects a younger version of her self-indulged mother. 'She ... tired early of her lesson-books' (*MG* 73), and seeks instead a less demanding world of romance, envisaging herself as an irresistible heroine. In keeping with this script, her Leipzig existence becomes a series of stage-managed scenes, where critical reflection has little place as she reduces life to a fictitious plot-line: 'Events and details, lighter than puff-balls, were to her links of iron, which formed a wonderful chain of evidence' (*MG* 131). Eventually the specious structure collapses to exhibit not Ephie's guilt, or 'a fatal frivolity ... of character' as Maurice surmises (*MG* 227), but the dangers implicit in her upbringing and attitudes. These leave her on the brink of retreating into a permanent nervous disorder, rather than enabling her to achieve an enduring sense of worth and vocation in spite of the 'uncertainty ... suspense, and helplessness' she has so painfully experienced.

The person who seizes the lesson, and is thereby laid open to the charge of selfishness levelled at independent, self-fulfilling female action, is Johanna. From the outset she is set apart by her inquiring mind. She 'had developed bookish tastes at the cost of her appearance', and her reading resembles Richardson's: 'Huxley and Haeckel, Goethe and Schopenhauer' (*MG* 73). At her mother's behest she abandons the goal of a university career and accepts the usual spinster's fate of opprobrium and family dependency. She becomes, in her callow sister's words, 'Joan the preacher, and Joan the teacher, and Joan the wise old bird' (*MG* 236). The revelation of Ephie's affair brings for Johanna the prospect of losing her role as chaperone and housekeeper. It forces her to abandon a stance of selflessness in favour of a career directed towards self-realisation, and this decision is confided to the novel's Simple Simon.

> Maurice realised that the girl was telling him a fact of considerable importance to herself, and did his best to look interested.
>
> 'Really? That's always been a wish of yours, hasn't it?' (*MG* 258)

Maurice's lame response indicates a failure to comprehend the complexities of Johanna's lot, increased in this instance by his guilty, self-centred concern for Ephie. Hence his final judgement on the aspiring academic, that 'she had been wounded in her own pride and self-love, and could not forgive. At heart she was no more generous and unselfish than the rest' (*MG* 261), is little more than a half-truth, and fully demonstrates the preceding comment that 'neither [he nor Johanna] had found the key to [understanding] the other'. Maurice would have her continue in uncritical devotion to Ephie — a view unlikely to be shared by an author who castigated the girls' mother for leading the 'vegetable existence' of 'a woman who has never been required to think for herself' (*MG* 72).

The character who receives the most penetrating psychological analysis is Louise Dufrayer, and she is the central figure in Richardson's reappraisal of gender norms. Intriguingly, the author makes her an Australian by birth, but does little to develop expressly the potential of her origins. Nevertheless, they surface as a partial explanation for Louise's actions, like her hunger for dreamt-of experiences like the European spring, or as a metaphor for the devastating effect of her fierce passion. More importantly, they make her to transatlantic eyes an unknown territory or blank slate, upon which they, unhindered by national stereotypes, are free to write the commentary which they imagine her actions merit. In general she is given a bad press by her peers as a woman of dubious morals and dark sexual urges. Even Madeleine abandons her normal reserve, under the combined pressure of jealousy and concern for Maurice, to assert of women of Louise's kind: '"Kindness and complaisance don't move them. A well-developed biceps and a cruel mouth — that's what they want, and that's all!" she wound up with a flourish, in an extreme bad temper' (*MG* 264). Here a mitigating authorial remark warns us that this is not the entire truth, much as Maurice's excessive partiality for Louise qualifies his dissenting judgements. As his first meeting with her demonstrates, she conforms to an ideal innate in him. She is likened to a 'corner of earth, happened on by chance, which comes most near the Wineland of our dreams' (*MG* 28), and her apparition causes feverish disorder and intoxication in his once calm breast. Henceforth she will call forth his idealising tendencies, thereby laying the groundwork for the couple's eventual tragedy, and for Richardson's much neglected critique of male romantic love.

Important clues to Louise's portrayal, and to its wider ramifications, are provided by Krafft. The most obvious is his persistent reference to Schilsky's mistress as Lulu, to which I shall return. The second occurs in a cryptic exchange with Madeleine, where the 'Bible' referred to is presumably *Niels Lyhne*, the work which, as Richardson confessed, 'stirred me as few books have ever done, either before or since':[22]

> as Krafft drew out his case to take another cigarette, a tattered volume of Reclam's *Universal Library* fell from his pocket, and spread itself on the floor. Madeleine stooped and pieced it together.
>
> 'What have we here? — ah, your Bible!' she said sarcastically: it was a novel by a modern Danish poet, who died young. 'You carry it about with you, I see.'
>
> 'To-day I needed *Stimmung* [mood/atmosphere]. But don't say Bible; that's an error of taste. Say "death-book." One can study death in it, in all its forms.'
>
> 'To give you *Stimmung!* I can't understand your love for the book, Heinz. It's morbid.'
>
> 'Everything's morbid that the ordinary mortal doesn't wish to be reminded of. Some day — if I don't turn stoker or acrobat beforehand, and give up peddling in the emotions — some day I shall write music to it. That would be a melodrama worth making.'
>
> 'Morbid, Heinz, morbid!'
>
> 'All women are not of your opinion. I remember once hearing a woman say, had the author still lived, she would have pilgrimaged barefoot to see him.'
>
> 'Oh, I dare say. There are women enough of that kind.'
>
> 'Fools, of course?'
>
> 'Extravagant; unbalanced. The class of person that suffers from a diseased temperament. — But men can make fools of themselves, too. There are specimens enough here to start a museum with.' (*MG* 495–6)

Commentary on this passage generally reads it as another acknowledgement of authorial debt to Jacobsen, or as foreboding preparation for the suicides of Avery and Maurice. Yet neither reading, nor Krafft's own predilection, adequately explains specifically female admiration for *Niels Lyhne*'s author. Unless this is attributed simply to fascination with a blighted, attractive young genius, its most probably cause is Jacobsen's insight into women's condition. Elsewhere Richardson intimates as much through her reference to 'Fennimore, sweet, tragic Fennimore, the most delicately drawn of all this gallery of women's portraits' in *Niels Lyhne*,[23] and where, she might have added, Jacobsen tellingly dissects the tyranny exercised on the beloved by male expectations.

This often unmarked oppression is highlighted in *Niels Lyhne* by two very different married women who have both learnt the cost of what passes for romantic love. The first is the worldly Mrs Boye, whose key discourse, from the point of view of Maurice Guest's infatuation, concerns the Procrustean nature of male adoration:

> 'this adoration is absolutely tyrannic in its fanaticism. We are compelled to adapt ourselves to man's ideal. Eradicate and destroy everything in us that does not harmonise with his ideal conception; it must be got rid of; if it cannot be suppressed, it must be overlooked, systematically forgotten and denied all chance of development. But what is not properly our own, what is foreign to our natures, is forced into the most luxuriant bloom by being lauded to the skies, by the constant assumption that we possess it in the highest degree, and by being made the head and corner-stone on which man's love is built. I call it an outrage upon our nature. I call it drill. Man's love is a course of drill. And we submit to it; even those whom no one loves submit — contemptible weaklings that we are!'[24]

Louise's unfolding relationship with Maurice is, at one level, an illustration of this very drill. She is required to conform to his ideal and chastised with tears or scolding when she does not. In the first part of the book Maurice consistently blocks out all information concerning Louise which fails to comply with his treasured projection. Later he impugns qualities which have no place in his imaginings, such as a love of dancing and vivacious socialising, in the harshest moral terms, and would 'eradicate' her offending traits. Jacobsen stops short of analysing the reasons for this recurring male behaviour. Weininger, however, took the extra step, and asserted that 'in all love man loves only himself. … what he completely wants to be and should completely be, his quintessential, deepest intelligible self, freed from the rags of necessity and from the lumpishness of earthly existence'.[25]

The impossible situation produced for women by male idealisation is also reiterated at the emotional turning-point of Jacobsen's book by the young wife Fennimore. Like Niels' own mother Batholine, she wed in the first intoxication of romantic love, only to awaken to the inadequacy of her mate and to the constraints which his unconsciously self-serving strictures have imposed on her. Now, like Richardson's Louise, she turns for solace to a formerly unsuccessful admirer in Niels. An intense but demeaning affair that grows more passionate 'the lower it sank' results,[26] as well as an outburst which reinforces Mrs Boye's critique and encapsulates dilemmas invisible to the male-centred probings of Nietzsche or Schopenhauer:

> 'Yes, that's right. You may rest assured that women are not such ethereal beings as many a good young man imagines. Their feelings are really no nicer than a man's, in fact they are in no wise different from men. Believe me, the clay of which both were formed was a little dirty.'
>
> 'Fennimore, dear, you don't know, thank goodness, what you are saying, but you are very unjust to women, to yourself. *I* believe in woman's purity.'
>
> 'Woman's purity! What do you mean by woman's purity?'
>
> 'I mean ... well ... '
>
> 'You mean — just let me tell you, you don't mean anything, for this is more of that meaningless delicacy. A woman *cannot* be pure, she is not meant to be — how could she? How unnatural! Did her Creator intend her to be pure? Answer me! — No, and ten thousand times no! It is utterly absurd! Why will you exalt us to the stars with one hand when, with the other, you must drag us down? Can you not let us walk side by side with you on earth as fellow-mortals and nothing else? It is absolutely impossible for us to step out confidently on prose, when you blind us with your will-o'-the-wisps of poetry. Let us alone, for God's sake, let us alone!'
>
> She sat down and wept.[27]

Here are insights which would have justified the woman of Krafft's anecdote in making a pilgrimage barefooted to Jacobsen, as if to a sainted oracle or shrine, and here, as Richardson no doubt recognised, was one of the best contemporary glosses on the problematic played out between Louise and Maurice.

Although there is no precisely comparable confrontation in *Maurice Guest*, Richardson relentlessly exposes similar well-springs of male affection. Maurice's attitude closely approximates Niels'. His response to Krafft's Nietzschean aphorism about whips and women is described as 'a flaming plea for woman's dignity and worth' (*MG* 165), while he is characterised from the outset as a dreamer, inclined to lose touch with reality, and proves this by idealising Louise. Also Schilsky, Louise remarks bitterly, 'liked a woman to be fair, and soft, and gentle — not dark, and hot-tempered' (*MG* 300). And the combination of self-interest, anxiety and wish-fulfilment which imbues these male imaginings is underscored by Maurice's actual dreams of love, that occur at crucial phases of his relationship with Louise. In the first, a woman advances towards him in a garden, offering him lilacs which she holds in her arms. It is a scene of archetypal quest infused with the lore of modern dream interpretation. The female figure assumes in succession the features of Ephie, Louise and finally the revulsion-inducing Madeleine — encapsulating Maurice's half-conscious feelings towards the major female figures in his immediate existence, as well as his own fears of ultimate inadequacy: '"You're too late. It has all been gathered," he heard a voice say' (*MG* 96). Later, immediately preceding his physical union with Louise, a vivid dream informs against his supposedly pure friendship for her. In it he can no longer remember her face, but only her alluring arm. This he mutilates with teeth and knife in an anticipatory revelation of dark impulses and a desire to harm that which threatens his own self-sufficiency (*MG* 323). Finally, with personal defeat imminent, he dreams of 'gentle comradeship' between them (*MG* 445), again revealing how idealising and self-serving impulses go hand-in-hand in male responses to womankind.

This implicit critique of ideal projections is only one aspect of the novel's concern with the disfiguring effect of masculinist stereotypes, summed up in the repeated phrase: 'Lulu is Lulu.' Louise's nickname is undoubtedly intended as a provocative allusion to the main character in the theatrical *succès de scandale* of the period, Frank Wedekind's *Erdgeist* (*Earth-Spirit*), which focuses on elemental sexual passions and the ravages wrought by an archetypal *femme fatale*, Lulu. It caused an uproar when performed in Leipzig in 1898, and was very much in Richardson's mind four years later. Then, during intense work on *Maurice Guest*, she recorded in her diary having read '*Der Erdgeist*' on 21 March 1901, and in 1902 noted having lent a copy to her sister Lil, with whom presumably she also discussed it. The play, with its controversial commentary on sexual relations, was obviously of special interest to Richardson, as were particular scenes. The prologue, for instance, which is delivered by a lion-tamer, depicts life as a bloody menagerie. He appears on stage with 'a whip in the left hand, a loaded revolver in the right', to the accompaniment of the 'sounds of cymbals [unter Zimbelklängen] and drum-beats from the tent'.[28] His accoutrements figure tellingly in Richardson's first novel, which for a time was entitled 'Tinkling Cymbals'; while the Richardson sisters would have been drawn to Wedekind's depiction of women's lot in Lulu. Named Eve, Nelli or Mignon, as well as dressed to suit her lovers' tastes or blamed for what she allegedly objectifies, Lulu exists for successive male leads as a fantasy object.

As in Wedekind's play, the nickname of Lulu is less important for what it tells us about the main female character than for the potential revelations it affords of the society which disparages her. In the first part of the novel, Louise is presented to the reader primarily from a male viewpoint, which generates conflicting female archetypes. To Maurice, in spite of the scenes he witnesses and all the warnings he receives, she represents immaculate perfection, whereas according to Krafft she is a dangerously seductive man-eater and whore, masquerading as female innocence. These alternatives re-emerge in subtly refracted form when Louise is sent to Dresden by Schilsky, supposedly so that he can compose without emotional interruptions. He is then shown justifying his behaviour and asserting his mastery over her to Krafft ('Do you think I'm not up to their tricks? Do you want to teach me how to manage a woman?'), and as proof a love-letter to him is triumphantly produced:

> *My own dearest*
>
> *Now only four days more — I count them morning and night. I am good for nothing — my thoughts are always with you. Yesterday at the Gallery I sat alone in the room where the Madonna is, pretending enthusiasm — while the rest went to Holbein — and read your letter over and over again. But it made me a little unhappy too, for I soon found out that you had written it at three different times. Is it really so hard to write to Lulu?* (*MG* 64)

Unwittingly, Louise's account encapsulates her sex's predicament caught between male-sanctioned stereotypes of virgin and whore. These have been thoroughly internalised — she addresses herself as Lulu — and become part of an institutionalised iconography, represented by Raphael's famous portrait of an alluringly innocent madonna. Physically there is little to chose between Raphael's ravishing heroine and Wedekind's, but allegedly objective viewers can find in their outer persons 'proofs' of contrary moral dispensations.

Louise, then, is much more than a Jacobsenian voice for normally silent womankind. Admittedly, she does at times assume this role, as when she lashes out against socially sanctioned gender impositions:

> 'Peace of mind! I have never even been passably content. Something is always wanting. To-night, for instance, I feel so much energy in me, and I can make nothing of it — nothing! If I were a man, I should walk for hours, bareheaded, through the woods. But to be a woman ... to be cooped up inside four walls ... when the night itself is not large enough to hold it all! —' (*MG* 121)

More importantly, she provides an extreme but exemplary case of the fate suffered by Ephie, Johanna and other women. The focus of a whole gallery of female stereotypes which serve to govern woman's thoughts, actions and self-imaging, Louise is figuratively dismembered by the male gaze in life as she was in Maurice's dream:

> [Her hands] had been photographed; a sculptor had modelled them for a statue of Antigone — long, slim and strong, with closely knit fingers, and pale, deep-set nails: hands like those of an adoring Virgin; hands which had an eloquent language all their own, but little or no agility, and which were out of place on the keys of a piano. (*MG* 213)

In short, she is relegated either to those concerned with physical as distinct from intellectual creation, or to the 'Wineland' of male dreams. These reflex strategies are essentially imperialistic, treating woman as an unclaimed territory to be dissected or impregnated in accordance with masculine desire — a New World full of promise ready to bear forth their fantasies. Louise's antipodean origins, in this sense, are particularly apt, and form part of a continuing concern with male appropriation which finds its best known expression in the Proem to *The Fortunes of Richard Mahony*. In both instances, the designated dominion is shown to have an identity and will of its own, and the male quester or would-be possessor becomes a victim of his own fantastic imaginings.

This comprehensive demystification of romantic love is complemented by an equally iconoclastic presentation of heterosexual interaction, whose main focus is the relationship of Maurice and Louise. It is sustained by fundamental dissonances rather than by compatible temperaments, and highlights the fallibility of gender categorisation. Though at times Louise is weak and excessively dependent, she exhibits that Faustian restlessness, expressed as hunger for change, intoxication and sexual piquancy, traditionally associated with male protagonists. She also assumes the Nietzschean whiphand, and pushes their relationship beyond normal moral categories of good and evil. The result is a gradual erasing of time-honoured emotional, sexual and psychological distinctions, as when Maurice accuses Louise of displaying 'a man's way of loving' by urging sober arguments in the midst of passion. Yet the lovers can also produce scenes of unbridled desire reminiscent of the following one from D'Annunzio's *Il Fuoco* (*The Flame*), which Richardson read carefully during the composition of *Maurice Guest*:

> Under the young man's hungry eyes her whole body clenched up again in the grip of a painful sense of shame. Desire for him tore at her like an open wound. She knew how much bitterness and impurity there was in his sudden excitement, and she knew how profoundly poisoned and corrupt he thought she was, weighted down by love, experienced in all pleasure, a wandering temptress who could never be satisfied.[29]

Richardson, however, in comparable probings of heterosexual perversity, avoids D'Annunzio's voyeurism and clichéd presentation of woman as temptress-whore, to focus instead on 'something irreconcilable about their two natures' (*MG* 334) — a something which emerges clearly from her couple's cumulative characterisation and in banal exchanges:

> 'At night, things get distorted —'
> 'No, no, one only really sees in the dark.' (*MG* 392)

Informing their characterisation is the same Romantic heritage which inspired the flowering of the *Bildungsroman*, now modified by *fin de siècle* accretions. In nineteenth-century German letters, night had been linked with a special realm of possibility: pagan, mystical, enigmatic, haunted, depending on the writer; while Nietzsche in 1872 re-envisaged the received antithesis of light and dark as the respective spheres of Apollo and Dionysius, and thereby provided a thematic treasure-trove for subsequent writers. *Il Fuoco* (1900), for example, foregrounds its author's debt to Nietzsche's *The Birth of Tragedy* through the Dionysian procession and intoxication of the Venetian crowd, as well as through the more intimate frenzy of Perdita, 'soaked in sweat, panting like a

Maenad after the dance'.[30] Similarly, in *Maurice Guest* Louise's later reinvigoration and Maurice's downward trajectory are mediated in terms of Apollonian and Dionysian forces. The Apollonian, identified with harmony, dream, order and the arts, is in effect the guiding principle of Maurice's dedicated existence in the first part of the novel. Related to his pragmatic northern temperament and his commonsense bourgeois notions, it is however endangered by his aesthetic and sensual predilections. For music, according to Nietzsche, is the exceptional art form. Capable of raising subjective consciousness to the level of Dionysian intoxication, it can efface all sense of individuality in a foretaste of death. In temperament Louise is Maurice's opposite, and embodies Dionysian impulses. She craves those heightened experiences which rend the veil of normality, and seeks the self-forgetfulness promised by death, or the utter self-abandonment characteristic of Dionysius's cortège: 'Louise, in particular, gave herself up to the rhythm of the music with an abandon not often seen in a ball-room' (*MG* 311). At times her actions recall the uncontrollable passion and savage deeds of the wine god's female followers, the Maenads, who in their frenzy tore Orpheus limb from limb: '[Louise] threw a wild look round the empty room; then, turned on her face, and bit a hole in the linen of the pillow' (*MG* 456). Though neither character is reducible to a Nietzschean archetype, their close approximation to these elemental principles underscores their irreconcilability, and the accuracy of Maurice's tragic realisation that 'the real truth, the last-reaching truth about her, it would not be his to know' (*MG* 470).

Their incompatible temperaments and outlooks make possible the novel's climactic reversal of romance formulae, when Maurice, and not the woman loved out of wedlock, is the ultimate victim of the conventional standards which they flout. A female, if not innocent and pure, is supposed to purge her errors: 'It was perhaps her way of doing penance; and, at this thought, he felt a thrill of satisfaction' (*MG* 280). But Louise, rejecting self-righteous, sadistic judgements, counters by accusing Maurice of wanting an effigy or automaton which will mindlessly conform to his desires: 'you would rather I was a wooden doll — is that it? How is one to please you?' (*MG* 314). Unlike the stereotypes enshrined in misogynist treatises, Louise has an independent identity and consciousness. These enable her to urge the inadvisability of seeking to bind free love in a registry office, whereas Maurice shows himself incapable of innovative thinking and condemned to misery by subscribing to the related cults of chastity and monogamy. His desire to find the beloved a *terra nullius* upon which he can stamp his dominion must always be thwarted by knowledge of Louise's past *grand amour*, leading to a 'constant fear, lest he should never be able to efface the image of his predecessor, which, yesterday, had boldly stalked out as a dread' (*MG* 465). Having transgressed but never entirely relinquished the values of his parents' house, Maurice will remain, as he belatedly recognises, 'a perpetual blunder[er]' (*MG* 437). Suicide, the traditional fate of guilt-laden females, provides a solution to the impasse, and his final preparations demonstrate inveterate adherence to the very code by which he stands condemned: 'He had no sympathy with those people, who, doing what he was about to do, left ragged ends behind them. His mind had always inclined to law and order' (*MG* 558).

This fatal inability to perceive and acknowledge his abiding impulses is underscored by the Moloch motif. At the outset, in one of the book's most enigmatic passages, Maurice dreams of an unavailing search for something of which he is not consciously aware:

> All of a sudden, on turning a corner, he came upon a crowd of people gathered round some object in the road, and at once said to himself, this is it, here it is. He could not, however, see what it actually was … At all costs, he felt, he must get nearer to the mysterious thing … (*MG* 13)

Suddenly the people run off 'wildly, shrieking: "Moloch, Moloch!"' And he, who 'did not know in the least what it meant', also flees desperately, as if from 'a malignant eye' or 'awful thing behind him', until he awakens 'clammy with fear'. The initial 'it' is apparently related to Moloch, but because it assumes the guise of a pagan idol, to whom human sacrifices, and especially children, were offered up, the dreamer is nonplussed. Partial recognition is lost or repressed. Attraction yields to repulsion, and what seemed life-essential becomes life-threatening. An actual counterpart to this vision is withheld until the penultimate chapter. There Maurice comes upon a crowd gathered around an accident, and recognises in its midst his bogeyman double, Schilsky. Desperately he fights to get a closer look at him, and then one stalks the other until, as in the dream, he is weak to the point of collapse and perspiring profusely. In place of the named but invisible Moloch we are now offered the concrete form of a man who has shown himself ready to destroy the childlike Ephie, or Louise whose fascinating eyes 'gave the face an infantine look' (*MG* 546). But this last perception, which immediately precedes the climactic encounter with Schilksy, is Maurice's. And rightly so. For he has subscribed to the stereotype of innocent womanhood, and thereby endangered the mental and emotional health of individual women. Ultimately the actions of Schilsky and Maurice are complementary and born of a single code, just as the composer in his dealings with females embodies impulses towards cruelty and domination which resurface in Maurice's unconsciousness. Understandably, the dreamer both recognises and represses this dark secret, in a psychologically complex action whose counterpart is his socially condoned reading of women as pure, simple beings, forever in need of male tutelage and protection.

In later years Richardson would seek to distance herself from the views and characters presented in *Maurice Guest.* To one correspondent she excused her protagonists' 'general unloveableness' as a product of the excessive heat and bitterness to which youth is prone.[31] And to another she argued the need to 'rise above hatred', and to discover '*some* good' in protagonists lest they 'fail ... to ring true', while admitting: '*you* might point to "Dove" in *M.G.* as an example of my not practising what I preach. — But I was very young in those days. I don't think it has happened since.'[32] Dove, it is conceded, is little better than a caricature, so that to identify him with conventional attitudes towards life, and to make him the mouthpiece of related views on womankind, is hardly to endorse them:

> By nature, Dove was opposed to excess of any kind; his was a clean, strong mind, which caused him instinctively to draw back from everything, in morals as in art, that passed a certain limit. Nothing on earth would have persuaded him to discuss his quondam friend's backsliding with Madeleine Wade; he was imbued with the belief that such matters were unfit for virtuous women's ears, and he applied his conviction indiscriminately. (*MG* 484–5)

Clearly Richardson no more approves the indiscriminate constraints imposed by conventional gender codes than does Jacobsen's Fennimore, and it is in the novel's constant, oblique critique of them that we encounter the main source of her youthful bitterness, which both subverted the traditional beginning of her *Bildungsroman* and inspired much of her later fiction. Student life in Leipzig, as Richardson knew firsthand, provided fertile ground for budding romances, as well as a staging place for new theories. Overtly her novel alludes to the struggles of Wagnerian against conventional music, and recounts the advent of radical teaching methods, introduced by the Lisztian Schrievers, which challenged the hegemony exercised by such patriarchal figures as Schwarz and Bendel. Covertly, a no-less-revolutionary perspective is afforded on sexual practices and gender hierarchies, though with characteristic discretion Richardson ends *Maurice Guest* on an apparently conventional note by announcing the marriage of Louise and Schilsky. Yet at the same time their union is problematised by associating Schilsky's success with Otto Weininger's writings. An art of balanced and seemingly impersonal narration was born, which would fascinate or frustrate future readers, and with it a way opened to less sombre but thematically related vistas in *The Getting of Wisdom*, which, as she professed, was begun in part as an antidote to the 'growing gloom' of her first *Künstlerroman*.[33]

3 Figures of Subversion: Cosima, Laura and Cuffy

'There is no incident [*Strich*] in *Elective Affinities* which I didn't experience myself, but no incident is just as it was experienced.' These words of Goethe to Eckermann are quoted by J. G. Robertson in his monumental *History of German Literature*,[1] and were familiar to Richardson, who confessed to having had Eckermann's *Conversations with Goethe* as her bedside reading over many years.[2] Moreover, she would have been struck by the personal applicability of Goethe's comment. After all, rephrasing Flaubert, she asserted that Maurice Guest 'c'était moi',[3] and it is agreed that traits of her father and herself are subsumed in the depiction of Richard Mahony.[4] Similarly, personal experiences feed into her portrayal of young females with creative temperament, such as Laura in *The Getting of Wisdom* and Liszt's daughter in *The Young Cosima*, who find themselves in societies which cast women primarily in procreative, nurturing and supportive roles — leaving higher imaginative tasks to the alleged lords of creation. Such thinking Richardson encountered during her formative years and mocked indignantly in *Maurice Guest*, and both her subsequent shorter novels are concerned with the extent to which women may realistically lay claim to artistic genius, as well as with the temperament and preconditions necessary for its unfolding. Related issues are also focused through her other favourite child, Cuffy, who is technically male but almost rendered sexually neutral by his youth. Through him the author explores an empathetic model of genius, distinct from that propounded by Wagner or Nietzsche, and the possibility of high imaginative creations that are no less demanding or true for conceding a place to those 'compromises and concessions, [that] pity and consideration for others', which Wagnerian art ruthlessly banished as specious, self-serving 'virtues' (*YC* 254).

Richardson's ambivalent relationship to received notions of artistic genius is well demonstrated in the short story 'Succedaneum'. In keeping with tradition, these issues are presented from a male viewpoint, in a tale which traces the efforts of Jerome Moçs to regain the inspiration which deserted him in the midst of preparing a putative masterpiece. Dubbed Saint Jerome because of his austere habits, Moçs is initially without a recuperative alternative to composition. Whereas his peers find relief from art's complexities 'in women's simple, unsophisticated minds', he, we are pointedly told, 'had still no use for women as a surrogate' and 'was still jealous as a girl of his immaculateness' (*EC* 238–9).[5] All this is about to change. First he pursues 'over half of Europe' a female performer known only from a faded poster, which bears the tattered name 'Bianca Josefa del S … '. Then he takes Salli, a young waitress who resembles her, as his mistress. Eventually he learns to appreciate other aspects of her character, following 'one of those long searching looks from man to woman, when every veil falls' (*EC* 259), and their ensuing liaison affords a bliss and contentment that temporally eclipse his artistic obsessions. Later he spends two nights with the 'phantom woman' of his dreams, the original Bianca. She proves to be a tawdry, appetite-driven figure, seen by him as 'a kind of *perpetuum mobile* of mastication, of talk', and of lust (*EC* 266) — a threatening actuality inferior to his imaginings. Nevertheless, this encounter marks the last phase of garnering life-experience upon which the fulfilment of his art depends. Up to this point he has remained, according to the tenets of a colleague, 'in the shallows' of existence (*EC* 244). Now he must decide between detachment, which is held to be indispensable by Sven, and immersion in 'the depths', represented by the pull of passion aroused by a woman. Moçs's final choice is for union with his art rather than with his young beloved, and the conclusion of the tale underlines both the grotesqueness and the elevation of Jerome's creative bent. It can trample under foot human emotions and yet create from them a masterpiece like *Tristan and Isolde*, whose *Liebestod* theme encapsulates the paradoxical nature of his vocation:

> In the corner of a shaded carriage, Moçs sat and listened to the grotesque distortions ground out by the wheels, now of this theme, now of that. And oftenest what he heard was one of a tossing sea, sailed by a ship carrying

> lover back to lover. In its broken rhythm, its restless upward surge, his own unrest, his growing exaltation found vent: he, with his face set once more for what, to him, had never ceased to be the one Reality ... all else but a ghostly surrogate. (*EC* 273–4)

Built into this male-oriented conception of creativity is a far-reaching critique which owes much to the example of E. T. A. Hoffmann. For not only did this German Romantic help to shape Richardson's view of the exalted yet difficult lot of the musician,[6] but he was an influential precursor in dissecting the bourgeois ideal of the passive, subordinate, self-sacrificing woman, and in revealing the blind egotism which ultimately made the puppet or automaton the preferred object of male desire. Parallels abound between his short stories and 'Succedaneum'. In Hoffmann's 'The Artushof', for instance, Jerome Moçs is recalled by an artist figure who pursues Felizitas, known to him only from a public reproduction, to distant lands, in a quest rendered problematic because his ideal is 'a mental picture which he could never lose, yet never win'.[7] This habit of male self-projection or displacement is pushed to its logical conclusion in other tales such as 'The Sandman'. There Nathaniel rejects his betrothed Clara, who is diminished in his eyes through her active intellectual and social involvement, in favour of the robot Olympia, whom he mistakes for a flesh-and-blood woman. Irresistibly drawn to Olympia's eyes, which seemed to 'gaze back at him full of love and longing', he is free to read all that his heart desires into her every gesture or silence:

> He sat next to Olympia, her hand in his, and, aflame with passion and enthusiasm, spoke of his love in words which no one understood, neither himself nor Olympia. But perhaps she did, for she stared unblinkingly [unverrückt] into his eyes and sighed again and again 'Ah — ah — ah!' — whereupon Nathaniel said: 'O splendid, heavenly woman! You beam [Strahl] from the promised beyond of love — you profound spirit, in whom my whole being is mirrored' — and much more of the same; but Olympia merely continued to sigh 'Ah, ah!'[8]

As Hoffmann's tale demonstrates, the actual blindness of Olympia's eyes has its counterpart in the wilful blindness of Nathaniel, while their interaction as lovers provides a devastating commentary on a venerable category of romances, and on what in women most gains male applause.

The recurring motif of eyes also holds the key to a critical understanding of Moçs's reaction to females and, by extension, to the tale's bearing on Richardson's artistic calling. His attitude towards women is thoroughly conventional, and reflects traditional poles of male response which, in *Maurice Guest*, were focused on Louise: it 'was one either of contempt or of exaggerated awe' (*EC* 238). The latter is epitomised by the name Bianca which he transfers, together with his dream-aspirations, onto Salli. Her real name, which contains a play on the French *salir*, to dirty or soil, is at first as unacceptable as her actual person and habits. Only her eyes, when not 'mutinous[ly]' denying themselves to his will, fail to disappoint. In them he discerns 'a strange inner light, ... some ancient wisdom ... which it was imperative he should make his own' (*EC* 252). This possessive drive is part of a continuing process of male self-aggrandisement, which began much earlier with Jerome outstaring passers-by of the opposite sex. Next he encountered the eyes of a life-sized poster which, in a subsequent dream, answer a deep inner need:

> they held a vital spark, a kind of spiritual promise, which none of the living had possessed: as if the unknown artist had condensed and compressed in them a sum of human experience. And gradually it began to seem that their message was aimed specially at him; as if these eyes were striving to make some wordless revelation to him, of mysteries in his art, in life, to which he had not yet attained. — And this idea grew till it became a certainty. (*EC* 242)

Thus Moçs succumbs to his version of Olympia, curses the 'witch-hold' this phantom of his own imagination exercises, and finally meets the young waitress whom he seeks, in effect, to reduce to a *tabula rasa* or blank slate: 'at the hard, stony, disbelieving stare to which he subjected her, her smile died out as if a sponge had been passed over it, leaving her round-eyed, open-mouthed' (*EC* 247). Salli is singled out to become his creation, his puppet. Failure to match his ideal is adjudged stupidity or coarseness. Her apparent non-compliance is likened to 'a wall of mute resistance', and contrasted with her volubility with the landlady, Frau Rosi. Among her kind Salli has a voice, but in the presence of the male artist she is silenced, and known only through his surmises: 'But her very dumbness spoke for her, and to him what it said was ...' (*EC* 255). The much-sought-after but finally threatening Bianca, on the contrary, is a woman who achieves self-expression with voice and body. To Jerome she verges on the demonic and must be fled. His course of action is finally vindicated by the returned 'gift of creation', and he is shown to obey the dictates of a higher power (*EC* 268). But what happens when these are felt by a female? Are other genealogies of genius possible? And how can a woman hope to trespass on a sphere so closely identified with male traits and longings? These questions, given the author's sex, are inevitable — though for an answer we must look beyond this tale to longer works which trace the transgressive acts of young women who aspire to be more than just a carnal muse or surrogate.

Unlike 'Succedaneum', which views the question of creativity primarily in terms of traditional male needs, *The Getting of Wisdom* and *The Young Cosima* deal with this theme resolutely from a female standpoint. The first is concerned with the struggle of a teenager towards career options normally closed to her sex — a state of affairs treated at a historical remove in *The Young Cosima* and shown to underlie the work's central drama of adultery and heroic female self-sacrifice. As such, these novels mark a crucial shift from the generalised treatment of genius in *Maurice Guest*, and the change is especially evident in the selected emphases of *The Young Cosima*.[9] Nietzsche, for instance, is a noticeable absence, despite his torrid relations with Wagner and his conception of a special code applicable to genius. Whereas the author of *Maurice Guest* would probably not have been able to resist depicting the clash of their influential world-visions, formal allusions to philosophy in *The Young Cosima* are restricted to an unnamed but 'great modern philosopher' (*GW* 248), whose work attracts Wagner in 1865 — the year in which Nietzsche as a student in Leipzig first became acquainted with Schopenhauer's ideas.[10] Instead, earlier interest in Nietzsche's masculinist code is displaced by an extreme sensitivity to and interest in her sex's potential role in a creative environment, as well as by an unspoken wish to make sense of the life of the dowager widow, Cosima Wagner, who for years ruled over the Master's legacy in Bayreuth with a will of iron.

Cosima embodies the predicament of a woman of great imaginative, social and personal talents, which are denied adequate and direct expression. The musical milieu in which her life unfolds represents the patriarchy in a heightened form. It is concerned with great masters and mastery, and the opening identification of Cosima, Liszt's daughter, as her father's female double ('I was met ... by your second self, *Maître*, your walking image' (*YC* 5)) raises the issue of what part she, as a mere woman, can be expected to play. The exemplary role available to her sex is enunciated by Abbé Gabriel, whose sermon is delivered with the full authority of the church and its temporal archangel: 'the life of a true woman ought to consist wholly of self-sacrifice, she herself stand for the "sacrificial offering"' (*YC* 42). But this role, the novel suggests, is by no means natural. Rather the attainment of even a semblance of this ideal requires years of rigorous training in self-suppression, silence and tractability, such as Cosima and her sister Blandine underwent: 'throughout their girlhood the news of them he [Liszt] had valued most was that they were grown tame and docile' (*YC* 57). Among the results of this regime are Cosima's general awe of male authority figures and the reduplication of its methods, as when she employs emotional blackmail to render her own daughter, another Lulu, manageable: 'The time had come to show [Lulu] that a superior will existed. To work, too, on her infant feelings by hinting at a possible withdrawal of affection, did she disobey or not try to please' (*YC* 166). Thus patriarchy is internalised and propagated, producing women like the sisters who 'once more, in strict conformity with their training, ... hastened to make light of their own wishes' (*YC* 45), and who ultimately assume aspects of Hoffmannesque puppetry: 'Like well-drilled automata the two replied as one' (*YC* 45). In Richardson's fiction, however, the spectre of Olympia invoked by male impositions is constantly interrogated by an appreciation of women's independent desires, and of the subterfuge or stratagems linked with their operation.

This concern with female will-power leads to the creation of a striking number of female protagonists with dominant personalities, and effectively to absolving Cosima of blame for adultery. Men, such as the weak and diminutive Hans von Bülow, are not only physically overtopped by their womenfolk, they are also frequently directed and eclipsed. His mother, the duchess, will be denied none of her long-held privileges, while his wife finally casts him aside in preference for true genius. Similarly Liszt stands in awe of his life-companion, Princess Carolyne, yet even she protests against her lot as a female: 'Ah!

if only *I* were a man — were you, Franz Liszt, with all your mighty gifts — instead of just a poor weak woman. ... How I would set the world ablaze!' (*YC* 16–17). As a socially constrained woman, her personal drive is forced to seek an outlet through union with male genius, a course which Cosima follows first with the gifted pianist Hans von Bülow, and then with Wagner. Hans, it is made clear, disappoints Cosima both by his failure to attempt original compositions and by his many shortcomings as a man. From the outset his sexual inclinations are depicted ambiguously. He is drawn to the image of Liszt in Cosima, he confesses to not being of 'the marrying sort' (*YC* 37), and we are told categorically of 'Hans having no real attraction to women' (*YC* 65). These indications of latent homosexuality are multiplied — and were subsequently confirmed by Richardson in correspondence[11] — until his role as progenitor is usurped by Wagner. And the case for acquitting Cosima at the bar of history is virtually clinched when she avows their complete incompatibility: 'we are perhaps two of the most ill-advised, ill-matched people who ever came together' (*YC* 223).

Her actions are also presented as a direct consequence of inadequate, conventional options for female self-expression. As Cosima's married life demonstrates, the 'sacrificial offering' demanded of her and other women consisted of unstinting support, obedience and discretion. It also required the combined skills of manager, nurse and hostess, and that a woman's personal fulfilment be achieved through her family rather than through intellectual aspirations. Even attempts to read independently, or to act the subsidiary part of copyist or translator, are frowned on by Cosima's husband and mother-in-law, because 'the best of husbands ... and a sweet infant ... are a woman's highest prize' (*YC* 164). The repressive upbringing which she shared with Blandine only marked the first phase of her education. Upon its cessation, she had unwisely dreamt of enlarged possibilities. 'She felt so strong, so full of energy: as if only now, the dullness and restrictions of her girlhood behind her, she was beginning to know what it meant to be alive' (*YC* 94). Like Laura in *The Getting of Wisdom*, she has still to undergo a series of rude awakenings. 'At first — I was young and ignorant then — I thought I had some right to wishes and opinions of my own. But I soon learned wisdom' (*YC* 221), or in the context of her essays at composition: 'But she had learned wisdom. This time there should be no bothering him in advance, with a subject that was still in the raw' (*YC* 124–5). Cosima will ultimately be set apart as much by her indomitable will as by her great gifts, for an essential part of her has escaped the full effects of the standard regime of female socialisation, making her appear at times, as Wagner remarks, 'like a creature unused to human contacts' (*YC* 158).

This latent, unspoilt core impels Cosima's struggle against convention and her radical insights. Like other heroines she envisages her marital ordeal in terms of physical and psychological incarceration, 'heavy of mind and of body', alone 'count[ing] the hours to her release' (*YC* 197), or more extremely as 'a Sisyphus task'. Potentially she is, as Wagner asserts, a free-flying bird. But the novel suggests that society afforded the independently minded woman, at best, an exchange of one cage for another. Cosima moves from home to school, to marriage, and finally to union with another embodiment of male self-centredness in Richard Wagner. She of course views the last stage positively, as having found true love and an object worthy of her complete devotion. A more accurate self-depiction, however, is provided on the eve of her great choice:

> Thus far, her life had been lived in a series of poky flats, with, for sole outlook, the stone fronts of other houses or the lines of a paved street. … She reminded herself of a person doomed to walk eternally under an umbrella, conscious only of the strip of ground at her feet. (*YC* 148)

This limited perspective does not prevent her from offering incisive commentary on what falls within her purview. Her husband is ultimately revealed to be an 'irretrievably second-class mortal' (*YC* 331), while she subjects motherhood to a brief but unflinching demystification: 'By now she knew just how much … and how little … a child meant to her' (*YC* 193). Childbirth is how Wagner envisages his acts of origination, and these are the only pangs of parturition which would fulfil Cosima. The fact that she was in many ways exceptional, as her family circle notes, does not lessen the implied social indictment; rather it highlights how massive the impediments were to truly independent female achievements.

Musical genius remains at once her natural calling and a path most surely barred to her. She has inherited the technical skill of her father on the piano, and his creative drive. Operating against their unfolding is Liszt's unwillingness to see his children subjected to public ordeals such as he underwent, as well as the alleged historical fact, unarticulated here but foregrounded by other writers such as Schopenhauer, of women's constitutional inadequacy to create original work:

> Neither for music nor poetry nor the plastic arts do they really and truly have sense and receptivity ... Nothing else should be expected of women when we take into consideration that the most eminent intellects of the whole sex have never brought forth and placed in the world a single truly great, genuine, and original accomplishment in the fine arts — nor for that matter any sort of work of enduring worth.[12]

As usual, Richardson's opposition to such assertions emerges indirectly, as when Cosima's efforts to lay the groundwork for an original composition are shown to fall short for reasons other than a lack of imagination or conceptual powers. Individual scenes and their distinctive instrumentation rise in her mind, as 'she began to have ideas of her own for the construction of a symphony, without, alas! the manly ability to supply a note of the music' (*YC* 98). This failure is the complex product of her socialisation. Not only does she lack formal training in composition, which was regarded as a male task, but she has been taught to avoid that expressing of the 'inmost self' which makes Wagner incomparable, and to eschew that other necessary attribute of genius, as defined by Hans, self-centredness: 'the creative artist's first duty is to himself ... *learning* to shirk, neglect, hold aloof' (*YC* 131). From woman is demanded stability, compassionate care, sobriety and indulgence towards others. Genius, on the other hand, battens on these offerings as its natural right, and insists on being 'perpetually in renewal' (*YC* 330). These strict gender divisions stretch well below the exalted rank of genius, and mean that even a 'musical galley-slave [such as Hans] had the right to slip his chains', whereas Cosima, with a telling sigh, is forced to resume 'her wifely task of greasing the wheels' which will promote male greatness (*YC* 150). Overall Richardson's depiction demonstrates that if there is something peculiarly 'manly' about genius, it is not the creative gift as such, but its sanctioned behavioural modes which are typified by relentless egotism. These run counter to a woman's deeply instilled training and to the permitted gamut of her public actions.

Denied creative expression, Cosima's energies find other and ambivalent outlets among the male contenders for musical genius. Hans, the 'lodestar' of her initial effort, is shown to be unworthy, while Richard has undoubted gifts but is also an exponent of that ruthless use of womankind which Jerome had to learn. On first being introduced to Wagner, we see him railing against his de facto spouse, Frau Minna, who has the audacity to voice her views ('God Almighty! why could women not learn to govern their tongues?' (*YC* 79)), and who fails to comprehend the 'sacred' needs of genius. Once 'exceptionally pretty' though now 'pinched and thin', Frau Minna has sacrificed all for him in vain:

> She had been through so many hardships in her day, trapesing at the Master's heels from place to place, toiling for his comfort on insufficient means; and her sole reward now, in everything that mattered, to find herself left out in the cold. (*YC* 87)

Also Wagner depends on women for inspiration, and to this role Cosima aspires. '*Tristan?* — what had *Tristan* to do with her? Not because of her, or through her, or for any love of her, had this supreme cry of human passion been uttered. Another — not she — had called it into being' (*YC* 256–7). The answer to her initial question is 'everything'. For although it is foreseeable that Cosima may assume her husband's goal of 'working for Richard, … for something greater than he is … than perhaps even he himself knows' (*YC* 89), this decision becomes inevitable on hearing *Tristan and Isolde* performed. Unmoved by Tristan's fate, she experiences 'a kind of exultation in which she felt herself one with Isolde; and in her, through her, made life's supreme surrender' (*YC* 90). Her great receptivity to music, coupled with deeply inculcated gender stereotypes, causes her to sink 'beneath the spell' of this model of 'life's supreme surrender' and, by extension, of its composer. Her immediate response to the performance is to be 'like a shade among the living. Or like an automaton, that said and did all that was expected of it, joined in applause, shed tears of enthusiasm, played the hostess, took part in animated discussions. But her real self was far away' (*YC* 255). Is this a testimony to trite reality transcended, as at the close of 'Succedaneum'? Or are we being invited to see in the effects of the opera a logical extension of her earlier socialisation and indoctrination? The novel sanctions both readings. The choice in favour of Wagner places her potentially in the thankless, sacrificial role of Frau Minna. Yet Liszt's daughter has more ample intellect and will-power than her predecessor. These lend a necessarily well-concealed dimension of egotism to her decision, for whereas Jerome Moçs can openly go to work as a second Pygmalion, Cosima must operate more subtly on her surrogates, and snatch what fame she can vicariously.

The clearest expression of this creative impasse comes when Cosima endeavours to find material suitable to inspire an original composition. Ostensibly undertaken to aid her hard-pressed husband, the exercise soon develops into an unconscious but unerring quest for self-fulfilment which illustrates familiar female predicaments and counter-strategies. Initially, following a suggestion of Wagner, she works on Aeschylus's *Oresteia*. The subject of a tragic, self-devouring family is foreign to the conciliatory temperament of Cosima, but not to that of its headstrong proposer. Yet work on it does reveal innate capacities, as well as the inescapable opposition between exalted aspirations and her proper sphere of domestic action:

> at moments so full was she of these ancients and their doings that they seemed more real than the paste she was rolling or the fruit she was potting. As time went on, too, pictures, great fresco-like pictures took to starting into shape before her; together with a distinct feeling for the individual instruments that might be used to accompany them. (*YC* 98)

No self-effacing Iphigenia, Cosima's genuine interest is kindled by the Trojan woman Cassandra, whose prophetic lament over her own tragic fate and the nullity of human aspirations provided 'a scene so powerful that she thought it must fire any composer's imagination' (*YC* 99). The element of unspoken empathy and identification is strong with Priam's daughter. Granted the gift of divination without a complementary power of persuasion, she was relegated to being an impotent spectator of male heroics. Instinctively Cosima is drawn to Cassandra as a means of objectifying her own dilemma and as a subject of universal relevance to her sex. And its personal applicability is underscored when her proposition is condescendingly praised and then silently dismissed by the anointed male composer of the household. Not entirely subdued, Cosima trespasses a final time on the domain of original composition. She proposes to Hans as an alternative

'*Merlin, a Music-Drama*', or a recasting of the Cassandra problematic in a more acceptable male guise. Yet even this common strategy of the female originator fares no better, leading Cosima to redirect her thwarted ambitions to the latest interpreter of the Tristan and Isolde myth, and to a scandalous romance in which the modern Isolde would eventually refuse self-immolation in favour of final dominion over the Wagnerian legacy at Bayreuth.

Cosima's dilemma is at once individual and broadly representative. She may be, as Hans maintains, 'the strangest compound of emotionalism and will-power that ever took woman's form' (*YC* 331), yet as the Cassandra analogue suggests, the grim lot of the gifted and refractory female is timeless in a rigidly patriarchal society. European women may no longer be physically stoned for adultery, but hypocrisy and harsh judgements make it still a real if metaphoric prospect, as when the maestro repays Cosima's devotion by displaying the thoughtlessness typical of Richardson's male protagonists: 'Though his words were like so many stones aimed at her heart, Cosima met the storm in silence' (*YC* 241). Wagner is pardoned his adventurous thoughts, sexual appetite and egotistical deeds, whereas Cosima's open courage in adultery is seen to transgress a sacred code which automatically sets her at variance with conventional notions of truth, as her cuckolded husband hotly emphasises:

> [Cosima] 'For it was there, when we were in actual danger of our lives from flood and storm, that I saw the light. Saw that truth was all that mattered.'
> [Hans] '*Truth? You* ... and truth?'
> [Cosima] 'Yes, even I.' (*YC* 324)

At the end, Cosima sets out under the cover of the elemental forces she has accepted, but in a world where she is still far from controlling her own fate. 'She had heard what she believed to be a "call;" had found her life-work. And whether she went towards it in joy or in pain was not hers to decide.' Yet as an earlier scene intimates, the drive towards female self-realisation is constantly renewed, and with it the possibility of changes to the inherited hierarchy of the sexes. The ingrained process of self-castigation and self-denial, set off in the wayward wife by an imagined resemblance between her child and husband, is sharply contrasted with the stubborn independence and untapped potential of their daughter:

> [Hans] himself seemed to speak from it [the child's face] — and with a long-lost directness. Oh, let her not be too hard on him. He never spared himself. Instead of sitting here thinking cold thoughts, she ought rather to pray for grace to understand, have patience, hold fast.
>
> But Lulu was wriggling to get free. Cosette loosed her hold; and, not for the first time, wondered who would guard and guide this little bundle of mischief, if she had to go. (*YC* 194)

Cosima's indoctrination seems fixed. We can scarcely imagine her throwing it off entirely, whereas this Lulu, called 'the wilful' (*YC* 194), promises like Wedekind's heroine to aspire after the more liberated opportunities available to Laura and her generation.

Cosima, despite her firm anchorage in an earlier age, is psychologically a sister of Laura, and her vital career choices depend on a tempering of romance with realism which Richardson presents as a specifically female problematic. It is accepted that Jerome Moçs, as a male, has freedom to move emotionally, physically and imaginatively. He can pursue his dream-woman at will, and indulge mentally in the great romantic vision of *Tristan and Isolde*. He is unhampered by the voice of conscience, permitted by tradition to use woman's love as a surrogate or enhancement, and at liberty to turn his back on quotidian responsibilities to enjoy final consummation with his art. But for a woman, as *The Young Cosima* and *The Getting of Wisdom* show, the myth of perfect love is usually a subtle form of entrapment which sees the young wife 'forced to adjust the rate of her progress to the steps of halting little feet' (*GW* 271). Hans von Bülow is told of Liszt's daughters that 'both their heads are running over with romantic ideas' (*YC* 9), while Princess Carolyne remarks that 'romantic fancies on the part of the young are soon got over' (*YC* 18). The Princess is of course right. Circumstances soon force Cosima to view marriage not simply as the great boon envisaged by the adolescent female, but as the pragmatic choice of a creative woman denied self-expression. Similarly, *The Getting of Wisdom* shows romance, and the imaginative capacity which feeds it, to be of crucial importance to women's lives. It exists in child and schoolgirl, in spinster and wife, and can be a source of delusion and escapism, or a promise and guarantee of a truly special destiny for the young woman courageous enough to follow her own star, as in the exemplary case of Laura.

This concern with romance and its ramifications is evident from the opening pages of the novel. Here Laura is pictured recounting to her siblings a fairy-tale of her own invention about a prince who comes unexpectedly upon a beautiful lady in a wood. Frequently the scene is read as capturing a phase of childhood innocence, which is about to be left behind when Laura travels to boarding school. More justly, it might be seen as a typical narrative opening *in medias res*; its preoccupations are developed, not displaced, by her later experiences. Already Laura has a long apprenticeship in the art of romance behind her, as her competent glossing of specialised vocabulary, like 'glade' and 'sward', and her unruffled response to interjections demonstrate. Furthermore, the fantasy scene, which will normally end in marriage and the happy-ever-after, suggests that she is well advanced in that process of socialisation which instils in young women the need to be fair and charming in order to capture a suitably adoring prince. This broader application is later confirmed when school-time is likened to 'purgatory before paradise', and a schoolgirl fiancée, we are told, 'was looked up to by the class with tremendous reverence, as one set apart, oiled and anointed' (*GW* 153) — or the equivalent of Laura's 'Wondrous Fair'. Finally, the scene introduces larger issues of narration and its responsibilities, of the hunger for romance in Laura and her auditors, and of the ways in which pragmatic concerns impinge on our dearest fantasies. These are recurring themes, while later scenes will indicate that this initial romantic plot-line is, in truth, a fairy-tale fit for the nursery, as well as a dangerous form of escapism which can corrupt innate gifts, and work insidiously to limit women's choice of vocation.

Laura's getting of wisdom affects her as a woman and as an artist, and entails a reassessment of these formative notions. She is introduced through her self-depiction as 'Wondrous Fair' and as a pedlar of clichéd romances. Successive disillusionments, however, dissipate her flattering self-image, beginning with the humiliation generated by her home-made, outmoded garments, and ending with the realisation that she is destined to play second fiddle to the developing good looks of her younger sister Pin. Similar disenchantment awaits her as a storyteller when she panders to romantic expectations. In embroidering on her alleged relationship with the clergyman Mr Shepherd, she flagrantly disregards reality, while her 'maiden' presentation to the Literary Society is steeped in past Gothicism:

> [Her choice] ended by being a toss-up between a play in the Shakesperian manner and a novel after Scott. She decided on the novel. It should be a romance of Venice, with abundant murder and mystery in it, and a black, black villain, such as her soul loved — no macaroon-nibblers or rompers with children for her! And having thus attuned her mind to scarlet deeds, she set to work. (*GW* 222)[13]

References to Shakespeare and Scott recall high Romanticism, as do the Ann-Radcliffe-like plot ingredients. Also Laura is elsewhere associated ironically with its self-parading over-sensitivity, as when no one is prepared to believe of her room-mate Evelyn, a mature schoolgirl beauty, 'that it could really be fondness, on her part, for the Byronic atom of humanity [i.e. Laura] she had attracted to her' (*GW* 244). The 'paper heroics' of Laura's literary bantling are 'a flabby fiasco', as are her initial, naïve self-imaginings. Temperamentally, Laura will have to learn to meet personal setbacks with Nietzschean, self-transcending laughter rather than self-pitying introversion, and as an artist to analyse romance in its contemporary manifestations instead of being satisfied with its trappings from another age — lessons which in fact shape the writing of *The Getting of Wisdom.*

This hunger for romance and the imagination's efforts to achieve adequate expression are not confined to childhood and adolescence, or to the embryonic artist, but are presented as a recurrent female need. Fantasies of Cinderella-like transformations, far from being limited to schoolgirls, assume diverse forms among the unwedded teachers. Miss Zielinski seems fated to succumb to the lure of romantic fictions. Christened Thekla (presumably after Schiller's tragic heroine in *Wallenstein*), she seeks release from the drudgery of school in Ouida's sentimental novels. Miss Snodgrass, like the independent Louise Dufrayer before her, contemplates a wedding of convenience 'in a kind of furious desperation. "I swear I'll marry the first man that asks me, to get away from it. — As long as he has money enough to keep me decently"' (*GW* 99). And Miss Chapman, who is placed beyond all reasonable hopes of marriage, imagines herself empowered in Mrs Gurly's position as headmistress:

> giving rein to her fancy, she could picture herself sweeping through halls and rooms, issuing orders that it was the business of others to fulfil, could even think out a few changes that should be made, were she head of the staff.
>
> But the insertion of Mrs. Gurly's key in the lock, the sound of her foot on the oilcloth, was enough to waken a sense of guilt in Miss Chapman, and make her start to her feet — the drab, elderly, apologetic governess once more. (*GW* 116)

References to the turning lock, guilt and authority evoke suppression, the inseparable complement of romance at school, and in the larger society which awaits the girls. For although the world preaches love to budding ladies, it underscores constraint or chastity, and marriage in *The Getting of Wisdom* is shown to leave females open to male tyranny and domestic slavery. Nevertheless, this imaginative impulse can survive cumulative setbacks, as Laura's mother shows. Her portrayal reveals both the origin of her daughter's gift and its potential trivialisation. As the carefully preserved keepsakes from her former marriage indicate, once rank, wealth and the freedom denoted by voyages to exotic climes were Mrs Rambotham's. But she, no less than the governesses, inhabits a society where worth is defined in male terms — as Laura's initial interrogation at school on her father's job and patronymic underscores. Stripped of her husband, Laura's mother loses the leisured characteristics and social standing of a lady. Her baulked imagination now finds an outlet in using her daughter's 'young body as a peg on which to hang fantastic garments' of her own conception (*GW* 101), which are as unsuited to present realities as Laura's self-magnifying reveries.

Richardson's critique of the forces which seek to keep in check these female struggles towards individuation is covert but unrelenting. Laura's upbringing reveals the constant application of a strict standard of propriety, which serves to ensure female subordination and to deny original forms of self-expression. Begun at home with maternal admonitions to 'behave in a ladylike way' and to be 'good and useful [rather] than clever' (*GW* 62), it is reinforced in school and society by a well-honed repertoire of exemplary condemnations. Their cumulative effect can be an internalised code, based on biblical and sexual taboos, which is applied repressively to unregulated female actions. Of mother's sewing, which constitutes an affront to fashion and aesthetic decorum, we are told: 'but there remained the matter of colour for Mother to sin against, and in this she seemed to grow more intemperate year by year' (*GW* 101). Similarly, the music Laura plays during the Strachey soirée is condemned as 'shameless', while a venial oversight, remarked when Laura is shown her sleeping quarters at school, is summarily linked with its putative, extreme consequence: 'an undergarment, lying wantonly across the counterpane' (*GW* 42). That is, laxity with underclothing is read as a sign of nascent sexual impropriety. Aggravated offences, such as Laura's Mr Shepherd narrative, Annie Jones's pilfering, and Chinky's misdemeanour, are met with ostracism: the punishment reflecting that the criminal has placed herself beyond morally sanctioned limits. The fear generated by this disciplinary regime is extremely effective. Even a rebellious outsider like Laura is not proof against its influence. Anxiety caused by ungovernable impulses makes her subject to recurring nightmares of expulsion, and draws forth the telling generalisation that, 'like most rebels of her sex, she ardently desired to re-enter the fold of law and order' (*GW* 209). Compelled to deny her own nature in favour of conformity, she is as surely debarred from being a Dostoevskian overreacher as Cosima from being another Wagner.

A major related problem, faced by an independently minded young woman like Laura, is to find an appropriate model of empowering and creative action. Typical female frustrations prepare Cosima to identify with Cassandra, a 'woman rich in misery'.[14] Jerome Moçs, however, can unhesitatingly grasp enabling parallels between his acts of origination and those of a divine creator, or Pygmalion-like seek to bring the creature of his dreams to life. Similar myths, when applied to a woman, invariably designate scarcely admissible behaviour, as when Cosima's unconventional deeds call forth masculine analogies: '"A wild man of the woods. Or Crusoe's Friday. O Master!" It was no use, Blandine was off again, her lovely laughter bubbling over at the picture of Cosette in such a rôle' (*YC* 158). But for Richardson this was no laughing matter, as is confirmed by allusions to Robinson Crusoe in *The Getting of Wisdom.* These mark Laura's passage from childhood freedom, where in sibling games 'she has been Crusoe' (*GW* 14), to subjugating tasks, including the casting into Latin of Crusoe's story.

The legendary tale, which to males offers an image of sturdy independence, inventiveness and dominion regained, leaves woman invisible, or forces her to identify with the enslaved. In Defoe's account Friday is a creature of an inferior race, whom man must ultimately save and discipline, and who assumes such stereotypically female attitudes towards Crusoe as adoration, service and domestic companionship. Similarly, Laura's immediate environment provides a variety of cautionary examples, but little more. Her exceptional classmate Cupid, who has fantasy and writing skills, 'went a-governessing, and spent the best years of her life in the obscurity of the bush' (*GW* 271). Even the revered Evelyn ultimately pursues the marital course laid down by romance. But as in the case of Cosima, an unsocialised core survives in Laura, as witnessed in her vacation pursuits of tree-climbing and 'long, solitary evening walks', and this, together with her intellectual gifts, provides grounds for hope.

Given the coercive, incarcerating nature of Laura's school-life, it is fitting that the most liberating model offered by the novel is evoked outside the narrative proper by epigraphs, drawn from Nietzsche's works, which head occasional chapters. Unlike Laura's frequent pose of Byronic outsider, these suggest the need for that transcendence of self and standard codes encapsulated by Nietzschean laughter and dance — a point underscored when Richardson acknowledged that 'the subversively provocative quotations from Nietzsche ... would light the way'.[15] Over half of these are taken from *Thus Spoke Zarathustra*, and of these most are from the section 'About Higher Beings'.[16] There Zarathustra dilates on the need to overcome narrow moral categories and current humankind, composed as it is of small and higher beings, so as to achieve its supreme form, the *Übermensch*. '"Man must become better and more evil" — that is my teaching. The most evil is necessary to the best of the *Übermensch*.' 'Incapacity to lie is far from being love of truth.' 'Oh how much better if your kind were destroyed — for it should always get worse and harder for you. Only in this fashion — only so does mankind grow into the towering heights where lightning strikes and shatters it: high enough for lightning!'[17] The eclipse of higher beings, the 'you' addressed here, is seen as a necessary prelude, just as mistakes, or that things turn out badly, are re-envisaged as ways forward to an as yet inconceivable development. 'Is it really a wonder that you don't succeed, or only partially, you half-broken one! Isn't there pushing and shoving in you the *future* of mankind?'[18] Richardson noted of Laura that 'in her small way the child came up against some of life's knottiest problems: crime and punishment; the workings of sex; passionate love'.[19] And she might have added to this list the issues and mode of progress that are dear to Zarathustra:

> Higher beings, you must overcome the small virtues, the small truths [Klugheiten] ... the 'happiness of the majority'. And how much better it is that you should despair rather than surrender. For truly I love you because today you don't know how to live, you higher beings. So, in fact, *you* live — best of all![20]

Many of the admonitions from *Thus Spoke Zarathustra* fit Laura's situation, as the epigraphs underline, though Richardson stops well short of suggesting that we see in her naïve heroine a prototype of the *Übermensch.* Clearly Laura still has much to learn, and *The Getting of Wisdom* drives this home with occasional scenes which read like ironic allusions to Nietzschean doctrine, as when Laura is said to have 'danced lightly away to her own undoing' (*GW* 228). Nietzsche's lessons, however, are appropriate to the eventual unfolding of her potential, which will require her to stumble on her way forward and to probe the essence of truth. Also his attitudes towards conventional and expansive temperaments are well illustrated by Laura's schoolfellows M.P. and Evelyn. Mary Pidwall is a fully fledged version of the local philistine. She 'was rectitude in person', Richardson remarks, and 'there were plenty such' (*GW* 181). Mary's conventional strictures hold sway over Laura until, 'with her refreshing laughter, Evelyn brushed these aside' — as if in illustration of the novel's final epigraph: 'Und vergeßt mir auch das gute Lachen nicht' ('And also don't forget good laughter'). Sacrilegiously designating M.P. 'that old jumble-sale of all the virtues', Evelyn underlines the younger girl's 'superior[ity] in wit' and boosts her self-assurance (*GW* 234). Furthermore, the relationship of these mentors to Laura's artistic prospects, and by extension to the Nietzschean epigraphs, is underscored by an earlier episode, from the time when Laura is seeking rehabilitation among her peer group at the expense of 'the rebel in her':

> One Sunday morning M.P. asked her to be her partner on the walk to church. This was as if a great poet should bend from his throne to take a younger brother-singer by the hand; and, in her headlong fashion, Laura all but fell at the elder girl's feet. From this day forward she out-heroded Herod, in her efforts to make of herself exactly what Mary thought she ought to be. (*GW* 184)

The comparison of this trivial scene to an elevated poetic succession gently ironises Laura's effusive reaction, and highlights implicitly what is not going to be advanced by prostrate adherence to M.P.'s moral vision: great imaginative literature. Laura apes Mary, and subsequently, while avidly drinking-in Evelyn's limited wisdom, sits 'perched, monkey fashion, on the side of her friend's bed' (*GW* 234). Such abjectness is as far removed from Zarathustrian self-reliance as it is from those self-liberating actions which denote a radical change of perspective: 'He who approaches his goal dances.'[21]

A crucial step in Laura's extracurricular education and Nietzschean progress is her discovery of Ibsen's *A Doll's House*, renowned both for its naturalism and for its affront to sexual conventions.[22] Its main protagonist, Nora, habitually performs the part of an innocent plaything to gain her husband Helmer's approval. She also suppresses her views in favour of his, as she has previously done with her father. Kept in a state of semi-childlike ignorance of the world, she becomes involved in a legal and financial imbroglio for Helmer's sake, only to see him brand her a shiftless woman and a corrupting moral influence. Apprised at last of her husband's selfishness, Nora rebels against life conducted as if in a doll's house. Grasping that her own self-realisation constitutes a duty as sacred as that owed to husband and children, she leaves home in pursuit of knowledge, fulfilment, and potentially social reform. Her future options are unclear, though the inadequacy of the pampered wife's role, the paradise aspired to by Laura's classmates, is glaringly exposed. Intriguingly, *The Getting of Wisdom* focuses overtly on the play's stylistic impact which rendered, in Laura's eyes, 'the most commonplace ... amazingly unreal' (*GW* 220). That this clash between realism and Laura's distortingly romantic disposition was also played out at a more personal level is only hinted at when we hear that Laura, who had read *King Solomon's Mines* in a single day, devoured *A Doll's House* 'on three successive days, with an interest she could not explain'

(*GW* 221). The reader, however, can easily surmise the effect of Ibsen's controversial matter on a young girl who is uncomfortable with the gender status quo. As a social and artistic *ingénue*, Laura has still to plot a path between romantic love and rejection of the opposite sex, as well as between melodramatic Gothic fiction and tedious, slice-of-life portrayals, represented by her first essay in realism, 'A Day at School'. *A Doll's House* points the way to Richardson's own later naturalism. It also provides a timely admonition on the need for each woman to develop her individual potential. In Laura's case this means avoiding the misapplication of important imaginative gifts which, though enabling tonic escape and the projection of divergent futures, can degenerate into an adolescent proclivity for 'shirk[ing] reality' (*GW* 207).

This personal dilemma is focused, and its resolution intimated, by the epigraph to the final chapter which underlines the gap that separates Laura from Nietzsche's ideal: 'None of you has learnt to dance as you have to dance — over yourselves and away.' Richardson's novel leaves us in no doubt about the applicability of Zarathustra's words. By its end Laura has had only vague glimmerings of her artistic method and vocation, while, far from being mentally self-reliant, she is pictured listening to the words of her departing friends 'with the deepest interest, and with the reverence she had learned to extend to all opinions save her own' (*GW* 269). Yet Zarathustra's admonition, in its original context, is proceeded by the comment 'what does it matter if you come to grief', and Richardson follows this Nietzschean cue by conceding that 'seeming unfitness [may] prove to be only another aspect of a peculiar and special fitness' (*GW* 271). Moreover, this intimation that the Nietzschean 'dance — over yourselves and away' has already begun is confirmed by a last resonant incident which fuses the main thrust of Laura's diverse education with Nietzsche's tenet. In a world turned upside-down by the departure of the schoolgirls, Laura casts aside the appendages of demure femininity, such as hat, gloves and lady's handbag, and runs off centre stage in a great burst of energy, 'the swift and rhythmic upturning of her heels' recalling the action of the dance. 'Lost to sight' she may be, but not to thought. The girl of the opening scene, so firmly under that sway of romance which would lead to lies and ostracism, to escapism and delusory fantasies, has been replaced by a free spirit, unencumbered by conventional expectations, whose apparently random course is compared to the sure flight path of an arrow. Laura seems *en route* to an uncertain but higher destiny, and this possibility becomes a virtual certainty when we recall another of Zarathustra's axioms from the section 'About Higher Beings': 'And verily, I didn't become a statue, nor do I stand there stiff, obtuse, stony, a column; I love swift running.'[23]

Richardson never wrote the sequel to Laura's disappearance, and when she next portrayed a young creative figure in Cuffy Mahony, he seemed far removed from her abiding concern with how women could be accommodated within inherited conceptions of artistic genius. But as Dorothy Green, quoting Plato, perceptively remarked, 'one of the interlocutors in the mind's dialogue with itself ... will always be a child' — an adage well illustrated by Cuffy.[24] Like Laura and her creator, Cuffy is capable of passing hours alone absorbed in his own fantasy world, and is rendered awkward, in part, because of his extreme sensibility. Its positive aspect is an instinctive capacity to empathise with others. This militates against the brutally self-centred drives revealed in Moçs and Wagner, and allows him to be genuinely sympathetic towards the opposite sex, in the persons of his mother and sisters. He thus represents a departure from Richardson's usual portraits of male genius, as well as a challenge to attempts to gender the nature of genius or, like Krafft in *Maurice Guest*, to present its manifestation in the two sexes as inherently different. According to Krafft, in woman genius is expressed through a combination of love and beauty, in men through creativity, with both having in common a need to go beyond normal moral constraints (*MG* 498–501). Cuffy's depiction cuts across established dichotomies to afford an alternative pattern of genius fully in accord with his author's life and work.

The seal is set on Cuffy's gifts by the brief visit of Baron von Krause, whose authoritative views provide a significant contrast with those attributed to his fellow countryman, Richard Wagner.[25] The latter's music, as experienced by Cosima, evokes 'another world':

> A dream world, that was yet realer than any reality; that, by the sheer intensity of its dreaming, turned the real into the dream. A world in which appearances were unmasked, pretences seen through: where stark truth reigned. Where soul spoke nakedly to soul, stripped of convention's veneer. — A terrible world. ... From the [remorseless] mirror here held up she [Cosima] would have liked to turn and fly; to put space between herself and the hideous reflection. (*YC* 254)

This 'terrible', confrontational expression is the counterpart of the unrelenting, masculinist conception of art identified by Hans von Bülow as a hallmark of genius. Its ruthlessly uncompromising projections recall Richardson's comment on the Master that 'his genius, his needs, his irresistible personality made Wagner an ogre who devoured without remorse the lives of all who approached too nearly', and contrast sharply with her own preference for nuanced, compassionate characterisation.[26] Closer to her own art is von Krause's praise of music which movingly captures, rather than eclipses, individual life in the natural world. According to the Baron, who is heir to the same musical tradition as Wagner, Cuffy's heightened empathy need not place him out of contention for the highest laurels. For the compositions of true genius are born of 'inward apperception', or put more simply for his young listener: 'it says what is in the heart, my little one, to each interprets the own heart' (*RM* 786). This doctrine, far from ascribing one set of attributes and productions to genius, suggests that they can be potentially as variable as human nature. The harsh light emitted by Wagner's operas is one of its expressions, but so too is the consoling music of 'the nightingale, and moonshine, and first love', which moves Cuffy to tears when played by the Baron.

Finally, von Krause also enunciates a specifically Australian program for art in which gender plays no apparent part. In a passage which draws on the German Romantic notion of a song inherent in all creation and the colonial trope of an unstruck lyre or unsung landscape,[27] he opens up a daunting yet dazzling prospect before Cuffy:

> 'Here is lying' — and the Baron waved his arm all round him — 'a great, new music hid. He who makes it, he will put into it the thousand feelings awoken in him by this emptiness and space, this desolation; with always the serene blue heaven above, and these pale, sad, so grotesque trees that weep and rave. ... But will you be that one, my son, you must first have given up all else for it ... all the joys and pleasures that make the life glad. These will be for the others not for you, my dear ... you must only go wizout ... renounce ... look on. (*RM* 787)

This creative program, rather than relying on the self-centred exploitation of others, demands the courageous, Laura-like pursuit of a solitary path, as well as detachment from life, or the capacity for renunciation inscribed programmatically in Goethe's *Wilhelm Meister*. For the gifted few, like Laura or Cuffy, art's realm is a special boon: a place of escape, free action and potential fulfilment. Yet as the ironies which distance Richardson from her artistic protagonists testify, she never forgot the potential dissonance between dream and reality. This awareness was daily dramatised by her rigid household routine and doubly insulated study, which sought to close out burdening, distracting actualities, and which facilitated detached probings and self-confrontations. Hence, when she set about realising the Baron's vision on a suitably extensive canvas, what she produced was not simply a new species of local novel, in so far as it dealt with misfit colonists or 'the failures, to whose lot neither fortunes nor stirring adventures fell', as she and Robertson underlined,[28] but rather another Goethe-like series of veiled self-revelations, or as Zarathustra put it more pointedly: 'Solitary one, you are on the path of the creator: you want to create for yourself a god out of your seven devils!'[29]

4 Re-envisaging the National Script: *The Fortunes of Richard Mahony*

The Fortunes of Richard Mahony is Richardson's greatest naturalist achievement and her most personal. Like Flaubert and Jacobsen, she remains ostensibly an impartial narrator, exposing the foibles of her main characters and refracting events through their eyes, while at the same time sympathising sufficiently with their motives to prevent the creation of a parodic, one-dimensional figure, such as Dove in *Maurice Guest.* Yet the material treated was close to her heart. In the central story of Mary and Richard she dramatised the lives and trials of her own parents, even going so far as to incorporate parts of their actual correspondence in the fictional text.[1] Like Cuffy Mahony, the author too had been lastingly marked by her father's public shame and dementia, and she now set about comprehending what she had once bitterly regretted. The result was a work with characteristics like those she attributed to Jacobsen:

> there is the realist's stern determination to face life as it is. But he wore Naturalism only as an outer garment; by temperament, he was more akin to the little group of psychologists, whose headstone of the corner is Henri Beyle [Stendhal], and again, there is more than one trait in his work which directly connects him with the old Romantic school ...[2]

In addition, the novel touches on many of Richardson's deepest preoccupations. Gender issues, spiritualism and eternal questions of the why and wherefore of human existence are prominent in this story, which interrogates fictional conventions, and attempts to offer a perspective beyond the yawning gulf of pessimism opened up by the speculation of such diverse works as Chambers' *Vestiges of Creation* and Schopenhauer's *Die Welt als Wille und Vorstellung.*

Richardson, by choosing to set her story in the second half of the nineteenth century, implicitly challenges comparison with other accounts of Australian origins, and with the national ideology outlined by contemporary writers.[3] With some of these figures, such as Nettie and Vance Palmer, the expatriate was in contact, while she was sufficiently abreast of local debate to be aware of the prominence being given to depictions of man pitted against the bush. These, later dubbed the Australian legend, focus on male will-power and stoic endurance, and on the close links forged between men when faced with inhospitable antipodean conditions. Still earlier, the largely male-scripted version of colonisation had presented the imperial venture as a bringing of enlightenment and civilisation to a benighted realm.[4] The barren, inarticulate landscape was to be rendered fruitful, oddities comprehensible and Providence vindicated by the God-ordained empire-builder, or by his more secular descendant, the bushman.

Richardson's account of local history in the trilogy flies in the face of these standard portrayals. Neither the founding settlement nor continuing encounters with the bush are taken as the seminal event in forming the fledgeling nation, but the gold rush. The digger, from being a simplified national archetype, is problematised, as are his acquisitive goals. Finally, the three-decker colonial romance, whose three-volume format was dictated largely by publishing conventions and marketing strategies, is answered formally by a novel whose successive volumes re-envisage the stock-in-trade themes of the colonial author. Familiar concerns with material well-being, with homecoming, with loving and transcendent vistas, are subject to keen reappraisal in *Australia Felix*, *The Way Home* and *Ultima Thule* — volumes which cumulatively locate a new charter or claim to the land, not in exploitative dominion, but in human toil and ultimate suffering which anticipates the verdicts of such recent writers as Patrick White and David Malouf, Judith Wright and Les Murray.

The Proem to the first volume portrays one version of the standard saga of national identity, and provides intimations of its silent ellipses. Superficially there is little to distinguish this opening depiction from the paradigms privileged by much 1890s writing. The digger-bushman is foregrounded, struggling against a forbidding land which can exact a high toll in madness or death, whereas woman is virtually invisible. Not until the closing lines does she gain belated access to the main drama, and then only as the alien other, or embodiment of those malignant, monstrous aspects which the country assumes to frustrated questers. This, however, is presented as a partial perception, born of an unquenchable 'unholy hunger' for 'vast wealth got without exertion'. A related critique of the myth of enlightened settlement is evident in the Proem's association of the gold rush with destruction and wastage, rather than with beneficent progress. Austral nature is portrayed insistently as pure before this latest invasion, and its true golden age is located in a period before this classical topos gained a distinctively materialistic range of reference.

> Under a sky so pure and luminous that it seemed like a thinly drawn veil of blueness, which ought to have been transparent, stretched what, from a short way off, resembled a desert of pale clay. ... feverishly disembowelled, and ... strewn with gravel and clay. The whole scene had that strange, repellent ugliness that goes with breaking up and throwing into disorder what has been sanctified as final, and belongs, in particular, to the wanton disturbing of earth's gracious, green-spread crust. In the pre-golden era this wide valley, lying open to sun and wind, had been a lovely grassland, ringed by a circlet of wooded hills; beyond these, by a belt of virgin forest. (*RM* 7)

Contrary to stock accounts of colonisation, it is dominion-seeking man who brings inversions, wantonness and chaos to the rich, fertile bosom of the New World, just as it is man who unnaturally buries himself in clay and gravel, blaming godhead for the ills that befall him, and cutting himself off from the larger pattern of creation.

Later, when these starkly materialistic vistas are subsumed within the narrative proper, this opening scene assumes an unexpectedly metaphysical dimension through the meditations of Richard. To him, Australian life represents a kind of death-in-life, or an unthinking immersion in material concerns. Its counterpart in the Proem is the lot of the miner at the Gravel Pits, who is buried alive in a collapsing shaft of his own making. As the focus gradually shifts to Richard's spiritual probings, nature is increasingly seen as a veil covering an unknown beyond. The ungraspable quintessence or barbaric she of the Proem, who defeats all men's puny efforts and holds 'them captive — without chains; ensorcelled — without witchcraft', is re-envisaged as a spiritual beyond, and designated 'the thing itself' in a climactic moment at Barambogie (*RM* 881). There, too, a prostrate man digs 'with his hand until what it grasped was a compost of mud and gravel', and he is duly 'caked in mud, soaked to the skin' (*RM* 884). But this time revelation, not death, is at hand, and as we shall see, the 'thinly drawn veil' of creation is lifted to reveal, not 'a desert of pale clay', but a great light and timeless vision which far transcend the temporal concerns of 'Australia Felix'.

To convey these antithetical attitudes, Richardson makes skilful use of Victorian gender conventions which were appropriate to her historical novel, but which have given rise to later misunderstandings. Her characters are, as J. G. Robertson underscored, true in thought and actions to their period, because she had 'with a rigorous and self-suppressing objectivity transferred herself back into it'.[5] Hence, for instance, bold speculative probing, which was traditionally a male preserve, is duly mediated by Richard, whereas Mary lacks a developed understanding of books, philosophy and cultural artefacts. She is essentially anti-intellectual, her sphere of action domestic, her interests mundane. These characteristics have been seen simplistically as proof of Richardson's failure to challenge sexual stereotypes. More plausibly, Mary's portrayal provides evidence of the author's studied impartiality, her refusal to create an ideal or unflawed character, and of a more complex design. For Mary's very limitations help make her the focal-point for a system of counter-values to the egotistical, acquisitive creed dominant in male affairs. Through her actions, she advocates the primacy of love and human relations, as well as demonstrates the importance of female friendships and her sex's contribution to nation-building. Moreover, although Mary expresses candid horror of feminists, their views are amply represented in the text. This is done either expressly through the words and deeds of diverse female protagonists, or indirectly through revelations of male exploitative economies, as when the vainglorious minister of Barambogie is moved by Mary's proposed improvements to his church and its finances to utter: 'That's the ticket ... women for ever! The work for them, and the glory for us' (*RM* 846). Outward adherence to Victorian gender divisions was compatible with their subversion, while it also enabled the author to achieve considerable detachment from deeply felt concerns. Yet as she admitted emphatically in her final autobiographical notes: 'I think it only fair to add that the person who knew me best [Robertson] always maintained that, in my imaginary portrait of Richard Mahony, I had drawn no other than my own.'[6]

A major objective of Richardson in this novel, as in her preceding works, is to explore untapped female potential and the realities of female experience. The subjects implicitly canvassed during the narrative read like a synopsis of the reforms advocated by suffragettes such as her sister: improved female access to education, rational clothing and diet, increased concern with childbirth and rearing, independent financial resources, basic civil rights and expanded career opportunities in an age when women were excluded from the legal, medical and political spheres. Similarly, myths of women's constitutional or temperamental inadequacies are exploded by a host of capable wives who surpass their husbands in the qualities which make for worldly success: shrewdness, energy, financial aptitude and practicality. The untiring Archdeacon Long is married to a woman whose 'energy … outdid his own' (*RM* 227), while Mrs Devine is as much a figure of unfailing vigour as Mary is of unfailing resourcefulness. Also women's natural career of marriage is shown to be no sinecure; rather it renders female self-reliance indispensable. In the trilogy husbands often fail as breadwinners or evolve into domestic tyrants, or as Tilly puts it: 'what we women put up with! There was poor old ma; she 'ad to be man for both. And Jinn, Mary, who didn't dare to call 'er soul 'er own. And milady Agnes travelling the selfsame road — why, she 'as to cock 'er eye at Henry nowadays before she trusts 'erself to say whether it's beef or mutton she's eating!' (*RM* 391–2). Little wonder she advocates warning women off men and longs for procreation without male partners (*RM* 889), while even the ultra-loyal Mary is finally driven to the brink of physical and mental separation by Richard's caprices. In short, romantic dreams of perfect compatibility are dispelled. And Richardson drives home the point with the games of childhood, through which the young prepare for adult life. Baron von Krause's visit leaves little enduring impression on Cuffy and his sisters apart from the name of Schumann. To them it is an empty signifier, which they quickly fill with the dominant reality of their own lives in a mock battle between the sexes 'of their own devising. They poked at each other round a corner of the house, with sticks for swords, advancing and retreating to the cry of "Shooh, man!" from the army of the twins, to which Cuffy made vigorous response: "Shooh, woman!"' (*RM* 788).

As in the book of Genesis, knowledge is shown to be central to gender roles and hierarchies. Women are repeatedly excluded from it, and still punished for its forbidden attainment. Unmarried females are not only faced with the spinster's fate of expendable service, but publicly relegated to a demeaning level of ignorance, which Mary's unwedded sister-in-law feels keenly. Despite a factual knowledge exceeding that of most matrons, this governess encounters a wall of silence or exclusion reserved for the uninitiated: 'here the speakers dropped into woman's mysterious code of nods and signs; while Zara, turning modestly away, pretended to count the stitches in a crochet-antimacassar' (*RM* 236). Married women are encouraged to see themselves primarily as promoters of male comfort and dispensers of supportive understanding. As even the intellectually unpretentious Mary learns, a minor departure from these norms can call forth a stinging marital rebuke reminiscent of that meted out to Inez in *The Getting of Wisdom*: 'It takes a woman's brain to house such a preposterous idea' (*RM* 339). Later, when forced to fend for herself, she grasps that success in the face of such gross prejudice demands 'knowledge of men and their ways' (*RM* 968). Or alternatively well-honed female arts, which render Mrs Marriner, who enjoys a beautiful figure as well as emancipated ideas, reassuring rather than challenging. She, we are told, 'had brains really equal to "gentleman's conversation"' (*RM* 604) — though importantly she knows how to revert to lulling stereotypes, whether by demonstrating devotion to children or by 'laps[ing] into some delightful feminine inconsequence'. This superior knowledge in handling men is drawn from an excellent library, as well as from the darker side of marriage and separation. Mary, who is capable of pardoning sexual irregularities ('in stories the woman who forgot herself was always a bad woman; whereas not the harshest critic could call poor Agnes bad' (*RM* 217)), reverts to current mores in the case of Mrs Marriner because of the threat posed by this 'bad woman's' growing sway over Richard, whereas Richardson invites us to see in Mrs Marriner a figure second to none in intelligence, but massively handicapped by social conventions and internalised codes.

This jealous hoarding of knowledge intersects with the issue of selfless and self-interested service. The latter emerges usually as a masculine characteristic. Evident in the ruthless subordination of women to male ends, or more simply in husbands' blindness to family needs, it renders 'manlike' a scarcely veiled term of reproach. Of Richard we are told, 'manlike, he expected graces and accomplishments to spring up of themselves, like wild flowers from the soil' (*RM* 716), while Henry Ocock 'manlike … no doubt imagined them living on air!' (*RM* 730). An alternative model to this shortsighted egotism is afforded by instances of female consideration and solidarity. These are often inspired by Mary's brave example, as when Mrs Rucker, the clergyman's wife, returns a brooch that Mary had sold in her dire need, or when Mrs Bowman returns unstinting devotion for the kindness Mary showed towards her when, as a time-worn woman, she was callously left at the mercy of the elements by a coach full of men. Far removed from male calculations of debit and self-importance, these actions are motivated by compassion, shared experience and knowledge of the human heart.

This strongly gendered divergence of perceptions is dramatically illustrated by reactions to motherhood. Fittingly, male self-centredness is exposed in terms of the Madonna cult, a male construct bolstered by religious observance. The appearance of John Turnham's radiant wife with babe in arms leaves the proud husband aglow with pleasure at this extension of his prestige and possessions, and Richard mentally genuflecting before a carnal embodiment of the Holy Family. But as subsequent scenes demonstrate, their response serves both to enshrine a dangerous ideal for female emulation and to elide an ordeal of which Ellen, a servant girl, learns to her horror.

> ''Ere, you girl, get in quick now with your bucket and cloth, and give that place a good clean-up afore that pore lamb opens 'er eyes again. …'
>
> Piqued by an unholy curiosity young Ellen willingly obeyed. But a minute later she was back, having done no more than set her pail down inside the bedroom door. 'Oh, sure, Mrs. Beamish, and I can't do't!' she cried shrilly. 'It's jus' like Andy Soakes's shop … when they've bin quarterin' a sheep.'
>
> 'I'll *quarter* you, you lazy trollop, you!' cried Mrs. Beamish … 'Such airs and graces! Why, sooner or later, milady, you've got to go through it yourself.'

> '*Me* … ? Catch me!' said Ellen, with enormous emphasis. 'D'yer mean to say that's 'ow … 'ow the children always come?'
>
> 'Of course it is, you mincing Nanny-hen! — every blessed child that walks. And I just 'ope,' said Mrs. Beamish, as she marched off herself with brush and scrubber: 'I 'ope, now you know it, you'll 'ave a little more love and gratitoode for your own mother than ever you 'ad before.'
>
> 'Oh lor!' said the girl. 'Oh, lor!' And plumping down on the chopping-block she snatched her apron to her face and began to cry. (*RM* 163–4)

Similarly, attitudes towards nature are coloured by the sexes' diverse interests and experience. Turnham, an exemplary colonist in his acquisitive, progressive orientation, takes 'jealous care of a transient bodily beauty' (*RM* 83), and argues that 'nature exists to be coerced and improved' (*RM* 115) — in this instance to bring forth the rare beauty of mother and child. Richard, as obstetrician, knows the facts of parturition, and should be well placed to sympathise with Ellen's and Mrs Beamish's reactions. Yet so ingrained are his mental habits and the rhetoric in favour of child-bearing that he conflates physical creation with its putatively supernatural ends. Hence, too, a man given to railing at local conditions can assert in the abstract that 'nature very well knows what she is about' (*RM* 115), whereas natural processes assume a far different aspect to the Mary-like doers. Despite social decorums and religious shibboleths (Ellen's curiosity is 'unholy'), they will find themselves eventually placed on the chopping-block. Yet this grim encounter can yield insights shared by Ellen and milady, mother and daughter. One is the realisation, even for a young wife like Mary, that situations exist when 'it seemed as if even the best of husbands did not quite understand' (*RM* 156). Another is an understanding of creative processes which envisages neither the coercion nor the transcendence of nature, but identifies her with abiding cycles rather than with the 'primeval monster' of the Proem.

This evidence of fundamentally different viewpoints and values is complemented by insights into the hardships inflicted on women by men's vile or unthinking deeds. These emerge primarily from behind the walls of women's conventional refuge, marriage, and assume special prominence in *Ultima Thule*. Examples range from a brief vignette at Gymgurra, where Mary 'with the help of an old, half-blind woman … swept and scrubbed and polished, in an effort to make the little house clean and sweet; to free it of a dirty man's traces' (*RM* 949), to Agnes's cruel treatment by her one-time lover and second husband, Henry Ocock. For the once desirable Agnes is reduced by alcohol and domestic tyranny to a brute-like level, where she 'lived on dully and stupidly, without pride, without shame' (*RM* 726). Now dispensable to Ocock, he is unmoved by the claims of past loyalty, and sends her overseas to die discreetly — only to be called to account for his savagery by Mary:

> It was of herself and Richard that she had meant to speak; of the tie between them which no living creature had the right to break. But Ocock's presence seemed to bring the whole past alive before her ... and memories of Agnes ... and of the murk and misery in which the poor thing's days had ended. And under the influence of this emotion everything came out. ... [She] stripped the veneer off his own conduct, laying bare his heartlessness, his egoism, his cruelty, yes, even brutality: how, in order to keep up his dignity, save his own face, he had wantonly sacrificed his wife, abandoning her when she most needed love, pity, companionship; shutting her up to drink herself to death ... Not a shred of self-respect did she leave on him: he should see himself for once as others saw him: and she went on, pouring out scorn on his hypocrisy and pretence, till she had him standing there as morally naked as he had come physically naked into the world, and would one day go out of it. (*RM* 966)

These accusations, although tailor-made to Ocock, wrench aside the layers of enculturation which separate the adult from the child, and which privilege each man, be he Richard Wagner or Henry Ocock, to treat those nearest him as chattels and expendable appendages to his will.

Within these broad gender divisions Richard Mahony holds a special position. His attitudes towards womankind are those of his age, and in him his sex's egotism is later heightened by his mental instability. Yet to see Richard as the covert target of Mary's denunciation of Ocock, as commentary has done,[7] is to misread his character. As Mary's crucial prefatory thoughts stress, her accusations fit the lawyer's relationship rather than her own. Heartlessness and cruelty are not in Richard's normal make-up. Love, pity and companionship are what he offers Mary for the greater part of their marriage, and if his conduct could be stripped of its veneer, then hypocrisy and pretence would not be the charges levelled against him, but rather pride, introversion and adherence to caste. These, coupled with his pursuit of ultimate truth, create tensions in the colonies, which climax in his last confrontation with the populist spirit of the times at Barambogie. Mary, trying desperately to resurrect his practice, has arranged for her husband to introduce the public address to be given by a visiting bishop. His Grace is a man of trite clichés who, in an age when 'old faiths lay supine, stunned by the hammer blows of science; and science had nothing soul-satisfying to offer in their place' (*RM* 558), has chosen to pander to local prejudice with a lecture on 'Our glorious country: Australia', rather than to grapple with unpalatable spiritual issues. It takes a modern Quixote like Mahony, with his intellectual faculties in disarray, to swim against the tide of disbelief. This he does during his introductory speech by testifying to his faith in an afterlife, and by alluding to 'ghostly' experiences. Derision and alienation are his reward, whereas subsequently 'the Bishop plunged into his prepared discourse; and in less than no time had his audience breathlessly engrossed, in the splendid tale of Australia's progress' (*RM* 865).

What especially makes Mahony an authorial self-portrait is this dogged quest for a reality beyond the materialist's purview, and his spiritualist convictions. Like Richardson he subscribes to the existence of identifiable individual entities after death, and believes that animals, such as dogs and cats, share heightened faculties with humankind. These affirmations, in turn, are part of their counter-case to 'the highest wave of materialism that had ever broken over the world' (*RM* 556). This 'wave' embraces not only the crude colonial enshrinement of wealth as a measure of individual success, but more generally a philosophical and scientific standpoint which attempts to explain the creation without recourse to spiritual agencies. To the venerable tradition of materialism, stretching from Democritus and Lucretius to eighteenth-century thinkers like d'Holbach and La Mettrie, had been added in the nineteenth-century evolutionary theory and biblical or higher criticism. Mahony encounters these in Chambers' *Vestiges of Creation* and Strauss's *Life of Jesus*, as well as the new self-sufficiency of science during his medical studies at Edinburgh. Yet its 'barren conclusions' (*RM* 467) can no more satisfy him than 'the vanishing rock of dogma and tradition' (*RM* 557).

These, like his carefully labelled collections of plants and butterflies, are eventually discarded in favour of occult studies and, in particular, of a supernatural realm made accessible through seances. The latter are subjected, with scrupulous authorial impartiality, to scathing criticism by Tilly and Mary, who amply demonstrate the abuses to which gullible seekers leave themselves open. Mahony, however, is allowed a last word which at once testifies to his unshakeable hopes and leaves the issue unresolved: '"There may be ... there probably *is* ... fraud. And why not? ... do not rogues ofttimes preach the gospel? But that there's truth in it — a truth greater than any yet dreamed of — on that I would stake my soul"' (*RM* 684).

Richardson inherited this legacy of doubt and, in addition, a related tradition of philosophical inquiry discernible in her allusion to the 'thing itself'. In context, this refers to an intangible and unreachable presence beyond, or perhaps underlying, perceived objects and experiences. The phrase apparently originated in Immanuel Kant's related conception of the *Ding an sich*. Acknowledged but uninvestigated in his *Critique of Pure Reason*, Kant's 'thing in itself' inspired speculation ranging from the idealism of Schelling and Hegel to the pessimism of Schopenhauer and the 'joyous science' of Nietzsche. These last two, moreover, figured prominently in Richardson's reading at the turn of the century. Her diary of 1898 in particular contains repeated references to Nietzsche-related primary and secondary material, as well as to Schopenhauer's central treatises, *Die Welt als Wille und Vorstellung* (*The World as Will and Conception*) and *Parerga und Paralipomena*.[8] In pursuing these researches she also profited from J. G. Robertson's specialist understanding of the period, as well as from standard studies such as *Le Mouvement intellectuel en Allemagne depuis 1870*.[9] Not surprisingly, this intense engagement issued in allusions to Schopenhauer in an early manuscript of *Maurice Guest*, where the German's pessimism seemed to find its fictional counterpart. But Richardson later played down the references,[10] much as two years after her mother's agonising death she omitted all reference to Schopenhauer in the summary of her 1898 reading made at the end of that year's diary. The effect of these decisions was to subordinate and suppress Schopenhauer's vision of inevitable suffering, whereas the nihilistic but affirmative philosophy of Nietzsche retained its prominence in *Maurice Guest*, and provided a metaphysical leaven in *The Getting of Wisdom.* Yet to entertain Nietzschean lore was, as Richardson well knew, to risk invoking the spectre of his master Schopenhauer — a point confirmed by *The Fortunes of Richard Mahony* which attests to the lasting challenge that Schopenhauer's ideas represented to Richardson's spiritual convictions.

Arthur Schopenhauer (1788–1860) composed his works over a period of almost forty years, but his basic conceptions remained constant. His major work, *Die Welt als Wille und Vorstellung,* appeared in 1819. Its seminal ideas were recast and elaborated in *Parerga und Paralipomena* (1851), which won him an enlarged readership and assured the enduring fame of his system. This builds upon what he hailed as Kant's 'very great' discovery — namely that we have conceptions of time, space and causality independent of empirical experience — to postulate the radically subjective character of human knowledge:[11]

> 'The world is my conception' — this is a truth which is valid for every living and knowing being, although only man can formulate it in this abstract, self-conscious fashion; and in doing so philosophical reflection is born within him. Then it becomes clear and certain that he knows neither sun nor earth; but always only an eye, which sees the sun, a hand, which feels the earth; that the world, which surrounds him, is only there as conception, that is, only in relation to another who conceives, who is himself.[12]

The entire world, described 'as an object in relation to a subject, a view of the viewer, in short, a conception',[13] is linked philosophically with Plato's realm of appearances, and with the Kantian knowable as distinct from the thing itself, and also with the Hindu spiritual teaching of 'Maya, the veil of deception, which shrouds the eyes of mortals, causing them to see a world of which they cannot say whether it is or isn't, for it resembles a dream', or a mirage.[14] Nietzsche, in his first major work, presented himself as a continuer and fulfiller of this metaphysical progress: 'Kant revealed how these [space, time, causality] only served to raise mere appearance, the work of Maya, into the sole and highest reality, and to substitute it for the innermost and true essence of things.'[15] Consequently, to attain true wisdom required, for Nietzsche as for Schopenhauer, a dispelling or raising of the veil of Maya — a perception towards which Mahony and other less exalted truth-seekers grope their way.

The second major component in Schopenhauer's metaphysical equation is the will. This is at once the Kantian *Ding an sich* and the will felt in each individual. It is the animating principle of all life, from the smallest crystal or plant through to the animal realm and humankind. Yet it is essentially one and indivisible — unknowable beyond its temporal appearances, a blind striving without cause and goal. Though not intrinsically evil, it lies at the root of human suffering, and the worldly endeavours to which it incites us are ultimately meaningless. As one commentator explains, 'will has no fixed end, which if achieved would bring contentment. Although death must conquer in the end, we pursue our futile purposes, "as we blow out a soap-bubble as long and as large as possible, although we know perfectly well that it will burst"'.[16] The notion of constant striving, elevated by the Romantics into the *sine qua non* of individual existence, proves to be a recipe for dissatisfaction and empty death. Unfulfilled wishes bring pain, while their realisation spells burdensome satiety, thereby creating a wearying cycle, blindly perpetuated by procreation, which gives rise to further opportunities for frustration and eclipse. In short, as Schopenhauer puts it, 'the subject of the will is continually on the turning wheel of Ixion, draws his water from the sieve of the Danaides, and knows the eternal thirst of Tantalus'.[17] Richardson encountered these doctrines at first hand, and her husband summarised them as follows, attributing a primacy to pain which is echoed in Mahony's profoundest meditations:

> The fundamental principle of [Schopenhauer's] work is that the visible world is only 'Vorstellung,' a creation of the reason, and the only entity, the real world, is the will; this is the active principle in the universe, and it reaches its highest development in man. But the will is incited to action by a sense of deficiency and by suffering; existence thus resolves itself into a perpetual struggle against pain.[18]

Within this cruel cycle, this long dark dream of human history, Schopenhauer allows for the possibility of moments of perception which pierce the veil of Maya. Through suppression of personal will or interest and complete self-abandonment, an individual can achieve a peaceful, painless state of pure knowing, in which 'we celebrate a Sabbath repose from the penal-labour of desire, the wheel of Ixion stands still'.[19] This is a condition of spiritual calm, celebrated alike by Christian and Hindu mystics in which, according to Schopenhauer,

> the storm of passion, the impulses of wanting and of fear, and all the torment of desire are suddenly appeased in a marvellous fashion. Torn free of the will, we give ourselves over to will-less knowing, and so enter instantly into another world beyond everything which moved our will and shook us violently. The emancipation of knowing [Erkennen] raises us as utterly and completely above all that as do sleep and dream. Happiness and unhappiness disappear. No longer individuals, we become the pure subject of knowing: we exist there only as the *one* universal eye, present in all conscious beings, but in mankind capable of being entirely free of service to the will.[20]

This blissful state is always potentially at hand, but even if attained, who can remain in it? As soon as the individual will reasserts itself, we succumb again to physical dictates. Then we 'no longer know the [Platonic] idea, but the separate things, the links in a chain to which we also belong, and we are once more immersed in all our grief'.[21] Maurice Guest's life-course offers no effective rejoinder to this dark vision, but Mary Mahony's does. For the trilogy bears the impress of its author's spiritualist beliefs, which enabled her to identify the German's cosmic will with a more purposefully creative, universal agency.

The human realm portrayed in Richardson's *magnum opus* affords in most respects a fictional dramatisation of Schopenhauer's conception of existence. Life is associated with suffering, unslakeable striving and the accumulation of unsatisfying worldly goods. As the Proem highlights, the New World, which is the contemporary embodiment of humankind's perennial dream of material fulfilment, will inevitably become the site of that individual disappointment, pain and eclipse, epitomised by the closing figure of a puny mortal as the helpless plaything of a nurturing, and yet malignant, supreme will. This fate is worked out equally among the rich pastoralists and merchant princes, the impecunious and the innocent. Representative of the settlers who conquered the land is the crushed alcoholic Glendinning. 'One of the pioneer squatters of the district', he has been led 'to drown doubts, memories, inevitable regrets; ... to the bitter discovery that forgetfulness alone rendered life endurable' (*RM* 212). Another warning example is provided by the hapless Bolliver, who takes Mahony to court on a dubious charge. Ruined after losing the case, his actions express an intense despair which puzzles a colonial viewer unconcerned by existential dilemmas:

> 'Gets outer court like one o'clock — 'e'd a sorter rabbit-fancyin' business in 'is backyard. Well, 'ome 'e trots an' slits the guts of every blamed bunny, an' chucks the bloody corpses inter the street. Oh lor! What do you say to that, eh? Unfurnished in the upper storey, what? Heh, heh, heh!' (*RM* 113)

With time Mahony, too, will be brought face to face with 'the innate perversity of things', as is his son. Generally a well-behaved boy, Cuffy reacts with tantrums to the inexplicable suffering of existence. In Venice he witnesses the cruel drowning of a puppy. Weighed down, it is thrown into a canal and bludgeoned by onlookers as it struggles to save itself. 'Finally, amid the laughter of the crowd, the flat side of an oar caught it full on its panting snout and terrified eyes. With a shriek that was almost human, it sank, not to rise again' (*RM* 690). The scene is a prelude to comparable, unexpected blows dealt out to the family when its shady fund-manager absconds with their wealth. The old argument of God's inscrutable purpose is, as Richard's use of it to Cuffy implies, fit to still childish fears (*RM* 693). Adult ordeals require spiritual consolation of a different order, such as is tantalisingly presented when Mahony and John Turnham move inexorably towards their harrowing ends.

John exemplifies the colonial preoccupation with the immediate, corporeal sphere, and the inescapable fate of humankind. Unlike Mahony, he has no time for 'effete standards and clogging traditions', and proclaims that 'grit is of more use to us than gentility' (*RM* 78). Likened in deed and gesture to Napoleon (*RM* 66), John represents an antipodean version of the career open to talent. The eldest of nine children, he lands penniless in the New World, but by thirty is 'a partner in the largest wholesale dry-goods' warehouse in Melbourne' (*RM* 66). Next he launches himself into the bustle of local politics, exhibiting a supreme adaptability as he lays aside 'his customary arrogance and pompousness of manner' (*RM* 261) to gain the popular support necessary to assure him of a place in the Legislative Council. Yet, as if in conformity to Schopenhauer's vision, all this cannot deflect an implacable destiny — a point underscored by the *Ernani* motif. At forty-six John is at the height of his fortune but greatly altered. 'Lean as a herring, yellow as a Chinaman ... he was now in point of becoming a morose and taciturn sort of fellow; prone, too, to fits of blankness in which, staring straight before him, he seemed to forget your very presence' (*RM* 566). These changes presage a fatal cancer. But before this unmistakably announces itself he makes a last determined assertion of physical indomitability. After brusquely claiming to Mahony that 'I am not aware of any decrease of vigour' (*RM* 567), he allows himself to fall under the siren-spell of the life-exuding Miss Timms-Kelly, and finds himself accused of having compromised her after a performance of *Ernani*. The choice of Verdi's opera is not random. In it three suitors vie for a single woman. One of them, Ernani, enters into a pact according to which his life stands forfeited to an older rival in return for support. In the final scene Ernani is preparing to wed Elvira when he is interrupted by the sounding of a horn, the prearranged signal for his death. In the novel it is Mahony, rather than a hunting horn, who conveys his relative's 'death sentence', and similarly there is no reversing John's fate. Even his fine constitution, which has borne him triumphantly through the trials of colonial existence, now serves only to prolong his suffering to insupportable extremes. Consequently, on the eve of death, his body and desire are exhausted, comatose, his eyes glazed. This is the nadir of individual will foreshadowed by his earlier blankness — only now it ushers in, not nothingness, but a beatific revelation. With his remaining life concentrated in his eyes, John is permitted to see beyond the diurnal veil the form of Emma, his deceased first wife. This of course is the vision of a terminally ill man; however, it is not undercut by suggestions of fever or faculties in disarray, but stands as a qualified affirmation of a possible afterlife.

John's end brings into sharp focus for Mahony the question of life's purpose. Just as Mary's discovery of Jinny's once prized shawl, now reduced by moths to a tattered rag, underscores the vanity of earthly possessions (*RM* 532), so Richard witnesses John forced to turn away from 'the material things of the world [which] had been his pride and his concern' (*RM* 622). The lifelong 'absence of the spiritual in him' leaves him facing a palpable void, which Mahony seizes upon as a representative condition:

> Life was like a procession that trooped along this perilous margin [of an abyss], brimful of hope and vigour, gay, superbly unthinking; and then of a sudden there was a gap in the ranks, and one of the train had vanished, had pitched head-foremost into the depths, to be seen no more — by mortal eyes at least. (*RM* 623)

He also grasps, thanks to John's ordeal, 'pain, as the profoundest of life's truths, the link by which man is bound up with the Eternal ... pain that bites so much deeper than pleasure, outlasting pleasure's froth and foam as granite outlasts thistledown' (*RM* 622). Against this threat Mahony can only muster Mary's forbearing love, since his wife decides not to tell him about John's beatific vision, and he feels compelled to probe the darkness of the abyss itself.

Although spiritual questing, or the desire to raise the veil, is firmly associated with an unstable protagonist, Richardson builds into the narrative crucial confirmations of Mahony's premises. Most frequently overlooked are occasional, but strategically placed, adaptations of Plato's allegory of the cave. It illustrates Plato's central teaching that we mistake our illusory life, based on temporal appearances, for the realm of real and eternal forms. This unthinking condition is likened to a state of mortal imprisonment which restricts our vision to mere shadows thrown on the walls of a cavern. Beyond it exists the Real, or the Kantian *Ding an sich* which Schopenhauer identified with the will. The first echo in the novel of Plato's parable occurs in Sheffield, the last on the eve of Richard's funeral. Trying to establish an English practice, Mahony passes a miserable winter incarcerated in 'a small, darkish room', cut off from the outside world by a 'brown gauze shade. Across this blind he saw people move like shadows; or like bodies immersed in water, only the tops of whose crowns shewed above the surface' (*RM* 448). For an instant, corporeal existence is reduced to shadows on the wall of his cave, and the insight is underscored in terms of watery submersion, itself a standard Neoplatonic symbol for the individual soul's immersion in matter. In Platonic terms, Mary is one such soul who has forgotten her eternal birthright. Hence, although at times striving to see beyond the immediately given, her profoundest visions remain, to change the metaphor, within the folds of the veil of Maya:

> How would it all end? — Letting her work fall, Mary put her chin in her hand, and sat staring into the flame of the kerosene lamp. But she did not see it. She seemed to be looking through the light at something that lay beyond ... something on the farther side, not only of the flame, but of all she had hitherto known of life; to be looking, in visionary fashion, out towards those shadowy to-morrows ... an endless line of days, that would

> come marching upon her, with never a break, never a respite, each fuller of anxiety than the one that went before. (*RM* 777–8)

This questioning comes to a head after Richard's death, but even then Mary's horizon remains stubbornly terrestrial: 'what had she to do with angels? She wanted the man himself, the dear warm incompetent human creature at whose side she had been through so much' (*RM* 984). The text, however, immediately provides a further perspective on her final meditations which reduces them to flitting appearances, generated by a loving though limited condition.

> She could weep, without fear of surprise, alone with him who had passed beyond the sound of human grief; in this little back room where, by the light of a single candle, monstrous shadows splashed walls and ceiling: shadows that stirred, and seemed to have a life of their own; for it was winter now, and the wild Australian wind shrilled round the house, and found its way in through the loosely fitting sashes. (*RM* 985)

The antipodean setting, like Mary's mundane hopes, seems to have a life of its own — but the Platonic subtext to the scene could direct the reader's vision to a realm where these appearances will be eclipsed, not by nothingness, but by enduring eternal truth.

Richard is the flawed but heroic spokesperson of this otherworldly perspective, and a major dilemma raised by the narrative is what credence can be given to the experience of a man well advanced towards certified insanity. Constantly restless, this latter-day Romantic quester illustrates Schopenhauer's dictum that 'all willing springs from need, therefore from shortage, therefore from suffering'.[22] Setting, as his mother-in-law quickly senses, too little store on the things of this world so dear to others, Mahony is always a victim of unfocused desire, feeling that life's pattern and purpose remain veiled from sight. In Ballarat, for instance, he decides after much vacillation to return to his original profession, and has the impression that 'all he had had to do was to brush aside a flimsy gossamer veil, which hung between him and his fate' (*RM* 178). Yet neither his career nor his metaphysical speculation brings about this disclosure. Instead, with his sanity crumbling, he gradually relinquishes society and its norms in favour of a maniacal fixation on private anxieties, as well as a desperate search for evidence of spiritual continuance. The resulting supernatural 'proofs', however, are usually countered by Mary's rational explanations, though his mental aberrations need not provide incontrovertible grounds for dismissing his conjectures. On the contrary, literary and popular traditions have long asserted the conjunction of madness with privileged wisdom or, as Herman Melville stated succinctly, that 'man's insanity is heaven's sense', and that by 'wandering from all mortal reason, man comes at last to that celestial thought, which, to reason, is absurd and frantic'.[23]

Richard's most exalted vision occurs at Barambogie, and significantly is counterbalanced, not by Mary's commonsensical rejoinders, but by Cuffy's less prejudiced insights. Here as elsewhere his innocent viewpoint affords an ideal means of conveying difficult scenes and contextualising commentary. Cuffy reads his father's night sortie in terms of the states of being lost and found, and compares him naïvely to two prototypes: the 'monkey in a wood' which the son pursues in an uneasy dream, and 'the picture of Tomfool in the "King of Lear"'. For Mahony, when finally rediscovered, 'had no hat on, and was wet, the water all running out of him, and so muddy, the mud sticking all over his greatcoat and in his face and hair' (*RM* 885). The dream image of the monkey encapsulates the father's return to origins and his physical reduction to the Shakespearian 'thing itself', which Lear identifies with a bedraggled Tom of Bedlam figure. Moreover, *King Lear* memorably employs the tradition of the holy or wise fool to unfold its dark vision, and to articulate the normally inaccessible. Its ingenious, allusive introduction into Richardson's text suggests powerfully that Mahony's revelation reflects privileged wisdom, rather than unfocused nonsense motivated by intense personal needs, and that he may be successively lost and found in ways which mercifully exceed childhood's limited experience.

The high point of Mahony's night venture in fact conforms to Schopenhauer's account of the preconditions for and actual moment of supreme revelation, but differs from it in affirming a divine instead of a blind will at the centre of creation. Before this climactic scene Richard has gradually cast off all links with diurnal reality and his ruling passions:

> His books lay unopened, withdrawn into their primary state of so much dead paper. And it was not books alone that lost their meaning and grew to seem useless, and a burden. He could forget to wind up his watch, to

> pare his nails; he ceased to care whether or no his socks were worn into holes. (*RM* 824)

The temporal is virtually rejected, although at this stage the life-instinct, that obstinate manifestation of the individual will, still remains. The next phase is self-loathing and suicidal impulse, manifested when Mahony rains down blows on a personal surrogate in the weary horse drawing his buggy. Finally, he takes two essential steps on the night of his ultimate vision: he overcomes the desire for self-preservation and then the impulse to suicide, which Schopenhauer maintained was the last expression of will.[24] This crucial process of self-transcendence acknowledges at the outset its metaphysical basis, and recasts the doctor's stubborn resistance to colonial materialism in terms of time and the *Ding an sich*:

> in his new clearness of vision he saw that his bloodiest struggle that day had been, not with the thing itself, but with what hid it from him. Which was Time. He had set up Time as his bugbear, made of it an implacable foe, solely to hinder his mind from reaching out to what lay beyond. That, he could not face and live. (*RM* 881)

The fear acknowledged here is generated by the unknown and by his awareness of mounting insanity. 'For, below the surface here, under a lid which he never lifted, which nothing would have induced him to raise a hair's-breadth, lurked a darker fear than any, one he could not face and live' (*RM* 828). Both spell eclipse of the rational self. Madness may well be the price demanded for Mahony's ensuing vision; the novel offers no verdict on this. But it does suggest that after such supernal knowledge there is no further cause for despair — a conviction mediated in a minor key when Cuffy closes the chapter with: 'What did it mean he [Mahony] said he *couldn't* be lost? Why not?' (*RM* 886).

Richard, having momentarily annihilated the last vestiges of his will, assumes the death-like position of the miner in the Proem to become Schopenhauer's 'pure subject of knowing'. Selfhood is overcome, and he shares the awareness of the German philosopher's '*one* universal eye'.

> he was lying, he found, in a pool of light; a radiance thick as milk, unearthly as moonlight. And this suffused him, penetrated him, lapped him round. ... All sense of injury, of mortification, of futile sacrifice was wiped out. In its place there ran through him the beatific certainty that his

> pain, his sufferings … had their niche in God's Scheme (pain the bond that linked humanity: not in joy, in sorrow alone were we yoke-fellows) — that all creation, down to the frailest protoplasmic thread, was one with God; and he himself, and everything he had been and would ever be, as surely contained in God, as a drop of water in a wave, a note of music in a mighty cadence. More: he now yearned as avidly for this submergedness, this union of all things living, as he had hitherto shrunk from it. (*RM* 884)

Counterbalancing Schopenhauer's vision of suffering as the bedrock of human experience is a sense of all-embracing union, epitomised by a suffusing 'radiance thick as milk'. Its restorative, maternal operation complements the Proem's concluding image of the New World as 'some primeval monster in the sun, her breasts freely bared, she watched, with a malignant eye, the efforts made by these puny mortals to tear their lips away'. Sustenance, both passages confirm, is never denied. But to the merely physical seeker no satiety can come, and existence inevitably assumes a malignant aspect, whereas access to its spiritual core provides an affirmative perspective on creation. Mahony's extraordinary vision is Richardson's version of what Schopenhauer dubbed the 'Sabbath repose from the penal-labour of desire', when, with the individual will annihilated, for the chosen quester the 'import of existence, the mysteries hid from mortal eyes, the key to the Ultimate Plan: all now were his' (*RM* 884). But the wheel of Ixion begins to turn again, and the debt to Schopenhauer's system, here answered and transcended, is acknowledged in passing when Mahony returns abruptly to the folds of Maya, and 'awakening found his brain of an icy clearness, in which no jot or tittle of what awaited him was veiled from him' (*RM* 884).

The closest earthly approximation to the all-accepting, laving radiance is the unfailing care which Mary displays in her dealing with humankind, and in her insistence on the good innate in each individual. Though presented emphatically as a natural woman who 'needed the evidence of her senses' (*RM* 706), she exhibits a charity and compassion of truly New Testament dimensions, and demonstrates that attachment to the loved beings of this world is far removed from simple immersion in its material shows. 'Her true mission in life', as Richard notes, was 'the care of others — especially of the poor and suffering, the unhappy and unsure' (*RM* 542). This, coupled with her fierce loyalty, defines the limits of her metaphysical speculation.

> Mary came as near as she ever would, to a conscious reflection on the aim and end of existence. ... in imagination, she gathered her little ones to her heart — and gathered Richard with them, he, too, just an adored and absent child — it came over her like a flash that, amid life's ups and downs, to be able to keep one's little flock about one, to know one's dearest human relationships safe and unharmed, was, in good truth, all that signified. (*RM* 695–6)

Her revelation involves encompassment rather than exclusion, the acknowledgement of communal before solitary concerns, and an unshakeable identification with those who share her pilgrimage through life. For a moment, too, her thoughts intersect with those of the freethinkers Tangye and Mahony. According to the former, the infidel chemist of Ballarat, 'life's only got one meanin' ... and that's to keep a sound roof over our heads and a bite in our mouths — and in those of the helpless creatures who depend on us' (*RM* 309); while Mahony grasps this humble truth during his ordeal at Barambogie. What separates them, however, is their response to this insight. Whereas Tangye posits that 'the truly lucky ones o' this world don't grasp it', and Mahony's thought sweeps on to transcendental union, Mary responds with unstinting mother-love to the stricken. Eschewing angelic promise in favour of purposeful action ('if *I* go to heaven, I hope at least to find there'll be something — something really useful — *to do*' (*RM* 684)), she nonetheless appears to be a terrestrial refraction of the universal principle perceived by her husband, while it provides an ultimate affirmation of what she stands for. The novel stops short of overtly confirming a vision of interlocking spheres — though it subtly evokes their union through the shared lives and insights of the two characters who most closely adhere to terrestrial and spiritual possibilities, Mary and Richard.

To the end *The Fortunes of Richard Mahony* maintains a fine balance between temporal and supernatural perspectives, between particular and collective fates. As Mahony recognised in Edinburgh, 'of what small worth was the individual: of what little account the human moulds in which this life-energy was cast' (*RM* 457). The thought recurs in a variety of guises, as when Richardson notes that 'the lovers passed, but the pledges remained: had put on immortality' (*RM* 74), or when Mahony retorts testily to Tangye's doubts with 'Pray, does it never occur to you, you fool, that *flowers* may spring from you?' (*RM* 307). When faced with the reality of death, few individuals can find relief in such reflections. Yet the book's *consolatio* relies on this vision of an encompassing oneness. It can be perceived on rare revelatory occasions, or in the daily miracle of sunrise, when darkness is dissipated and the mind's eye drawn towards infinity:

> And now the sky was streaked with crimson-madder; the last clouds scattered, drenched in orange and rose, and flames burned in the glass of every window-pane. Up came the tip of the sun's rim, grew to a fiery quarter, to a half; till, bounding free from the horizon, it began to mount and to lose its girth in the immensity of the sky. (*RM* 199–200)

Less exaltedly, the novel ends with Richard's interment, but Mary's earthly sorrow does not predominate. Instead, emphasis falls on a grave-site 'where not a tree, not a bush, nor even a fence stands to break [the winds'] force. Or to limit the outlook', and on reconciling, fruitful union: 'The rich and kindly earth of his adopted country absorbed his perishable body, as the country itself had never contrived to make its own, his wayward, vagrant spirit' (*RM* 990). As in the Proem, the smallness and nullity of human endeavours in comparison with the scale of antipodean nature are underscored, though this time quester and other are subsumed in a sense of abiding wholeness which ratifies both the role of the veil of Maya and all our puny efforts to attain an unlimited prospect.

5 Parables of Identity: 'Growing Pains' and other stories

Created largely in the shadow of *The Fortunes of Richard Mahony*, Richardson's shorter fiction has received an undeservedly cool reception from publishers and critics alike. Commentary has often treated it as being of strictly minor or secondary importance compared with her novels,[1] and the author, although drawn to the more condensed form, claimed that market forces obliged her to concentrate her energies elsewhere: 'if you had gone through the schooling I have — found it *absolutely impossible* to place a short story — you would not have wasted much of your time on trying to write them either. It seemed wiser to stick to the big works which I knew I could get published.'[2] The craft involved in the writing of long and shorter works, however, was similar, as are their thematic concerns. Avoiding direct polemic in favour of restraint and resonantly depicted scenes, she translated private into seemingly impersonal observations, and yet was ready to acknowledge that 'from enduring one's own personal griefs and pains one knows those of others'.[3] The origin of her shorter pieces is diverse. Certain tales are traceable to crucial events which affected her, such as 'Mary Christina', born of her mother's tortured death from cancer of the colon, or her German tales, which draw on over a decade's experience in that country. More complexly, the eight or nine story sequence 'Growing Pains' affords an intricate critique of female enculturation. Indeed, so radical are these reflections that Richardson apparently felt uneasy about the original suite of eight stories that ended with her bold account of lesbian longing in 'Two Hanged Women'. In later life she wished to add to it the more orthodoxly heterosexual configuration found in 'Sister Ann'[4] — though even this is not without that 'sting in its tail' (*EC* 265) which is a hallmark of the author of *The Getting of Wisdom*. The richness and complexity of the stories invite many approaches. Mine is to treat them as a summation of their author's abiding concerns, beginning with her prophetic account of German society in 'The Professor's Experiment', and moving, via the appropriation of supernatural motifs to critical ends in 'Mary Christina' and 'The Coat', to the cumulative verdict passed on gender formation in 'Growing Pains: Sketches of Girlhood'.

Richardson's ambivalent response to Germany, which she knew so intimately, is given enduring form in 'The Professor's Experiment'. Most obviously the tale complements the critique of German misogyny launched in *Maurice Guest*, depicting male chauvinism and boundless egotism embodied by the physically unappetising Paulchen. This pedant exploits first his sister to further his career and then, once this is assured, seeks to replace her with a younger and more intimate domestic figure who will adorn his life, add comfort to his surroundings, and provide projections of his authority in the form of obedient offspring. Yet the same self-interested character, who demands a perfectly regulated existence, a secure and undisturbed study, and 'prized above all else the peace and tranquillity necessary to mental production' (*EC* 212), contains elements of authorial self-parody, while his chosen career as philologist recalls that of J. G. Robertson. Richardson was clearly aware of the dangers and excesses to which their intellectual vocations were liable; however, a sharp distinction needs to be made between Paulchen's devoted but essentially unprofitable labours on the 'Oscan Declension' and the far more fruitful and less humanly hostile publishing careers of Richardson and her husband. More generally, the story attests to Ettie's negative attitude to certain aspects of German life. Although it provided her with intellectual impulses and a cultural wealth crucial to her entire career, she also identified it with 'a streak of brutality' and political immaturity,[5] which helped make possible major European wars and the rise of National Socialism. About the latter, at a time when others were 'kowtowing [to] & handshaking' with the Brown Shirts, Richardson had no illusions. In 1938 she asserted that 'one can't be friends with a lunatic', and a year later she clearsightedly linked 'Hitler & his gang' with 'nihilism pure & simple', and with having 'set in motion *a ruin of the national character* on a scale hitherto unimaginable'.[6] Yet to certain observers it was far from unimaginable, and a less modest writer might have remarked that the 'seeds' for the fall of what was 'once the most cultured land in Europe' are already discernible in 'The Professor's Experiment'.[7]

Paulchen, and the social critique of which he is the focus, should be seen alongside Heinrich Mann's more famous attacks on the mentality fostered by Wilhelminian Germany. In *Professor Unrat* (1905), for instance,[8] which achieved international renown when filmed as *Der Blaue Engel* (*The Blue Angel*), he deals with a similarly withered pedagogue, and the mindless obedience to routine and duty which lent itself to totalitarian dictates. This national dimension is more fully explored in later novels such as *Der Untertan* (1918). There Mann's viewpoint is encapsulated by the independently minded Buck, who refuses to yield an inch of intellectual ground to Diederich's physical threats and blustering rhetoric:

> The future? That is precisely the subject of confusion. The national moment [Tat] has moved on [abgehaust] in the course of a hundred years. What we are experiencing and will continue to experience are its twitchings and the odour of its corpse. There won't be any wholesome air.[9]

Women in this realm are ruthlessly subdued. Valued primarily for their reproductive and familial functions, independent desires are viewed as 'frivolities and improprieties', their persons as expendable for the good of the race.[10] In childhood and youth Diederich uses females to practise his claims to power in society, and later asserts as infallible his rights to sexual dominion. Even the nocturnal rebellions of his wife Guste, which see her beat, humiliate and exploit him physically, only reduplicate the pervasive pattern of male domination, so that each day, with crushing inevitability, 'authority and custom triumphed again'.[11]

Richardson's criticism of the national character is hardly less sweeping, though she offers a more sympathetic presentation of that most neglected of German resources — *die deutsche Frau.* Paulchen's household reflects his country's veneration of duty, sobriety, punctuality, learning, order and routine. The unfolding narrative, however, reveals that disorder and breaches of discipline are despised because of an underlying terror of change, and that the impeccably regulated domestic machinery precludes spontaneity and natural grace by reducing all to 'a monotony, a dead level of dullness, that passed belief' (*EC* 213). This 'soulless exactitude', in turn, ensures social cohesion. It rigorously enforces the *Untertan* or subject mentality which rendered Germany a hierarchical society built around dominance and subjugation, where each level imposes the same tyrannical pattern on those beneath it. Alternate kowtowing and bullying produces individuals with neither initiative nor deeply held personal values, who are virtually helpless before a threat or the state's ultimate authority. Thus Annemarie in a sense dominates Paulchen, and he his new wife Elsa, who by a happy coincidence bears the same maiden name as Hitler's mistress Eva Braun. Each secretly smarts under these oppressive conditions and longs to rebel. Also the pedant-manikin, whose stratagems of power are pushed to parodic lengths in his jealous hoarding of the daily paper and his oppressive cultivation of foreign tongues, turns to water when faced with an unceremonious midwife, or with a refractory and sensual housemaid. Instead of confronting Marthe and her putative lover, Paulchen prefers to resort to underhand ploys, and the affair quickly assumes 'a morbid interest for him' which sweeps aside his pedagogic calling. He and Professor Unrat are from the same mould, with Richardson departing from Mann's model when she challenges the reader to shift from the conventional view of Annemarie as a dour, domineering spinster to see in her a potential source of reforming impulse.

While underscoring the thankless lot of the German *Hausfrau*, the tale also demonstrates that both sexes require liberation from their unthinking roles. Subtle parallels are established between husband and wife. The clothes of each, for instance, evoke comparisons with the plastic arts. His baggy apparel 'had as little pretence to form as the rest of him, and continued a series of transverse lines which, in their prodigality, would have delighted a Dürer' (*EC* 85). Her movements are likened to those of 'slim, fleet, dancing figures on vase or frieze ... Against her, as she went, a many-folded drapery should have flattened or swayed' (*EC* 98). Characteristically, these pointed asides identify him with empty forms, and Elsa with an authorial wish for a finer, freer destiny. Similarly, his labours on the 'Oscan declension' have their counterpart in her ceaseless stitching of a trousseau — a point underscored by their respective birth-pangs and products at the close of the tale. And again the analogies work against the professor. He affords a travesty of life and creativity; his wife tastes their mystery and bitterness to the full. Nevertheless, Richardson is adamant that the three main characters are modern versions of the automatons singled out by Hoffmann to designate regimented, bloodless, Prussian society:

> Their programme never varied; was repeated week after week, month after month, till it began to seem to Elsa that the three of them were mere clockwork figures, wound up to perform a series of mechanical actions. With words that fitted these, and appropriate doll-like gestures. (*EC* 211)

Male self-interest and the institutional structures which propagate it emerge here as the 'fetish, this Moloch', and womankind, conditioned to unfailing service and self-effacement, as its primary victim. Only Annemarie, who has never married, harbours a nonconformist streak, and gradually her very oddness suggests a Laura-like sense of election or egregious destiny. Initially we are told that she was not 'the stuff of which human sacrifices are made' (*EC* 196). Then she is boldly refigured as alone standing 'for revolution, for a violent break with tradition' (*EC* 204). Finally and most menacingly, she is depicted as mentally emancipated behind a façade of domestic embroidering, rejecting the role of automaton or figurehead, and aspiring towards self-realisation in an apartment which has become, and been seen for, the living tomb it always was. Richardson-like, 'behind her locked door, Annemarie continued to indulge thoughts and hatch plans of the kind that herald revolutions' (*EC* 233).

Although Annemarie may bitterly regret her exclusion from normal life, the overall verdict of Richardson's stories is of existence as a potential vale of tears or place of entrapment rather than an earthly paradise. Frequently there is a spiritualist, even Platonic, dimension to her tales. Peterle Lüthy is described as 'a tiny prisoner to life' (*EC* 156) and, most starkly, 'Mary Christina' uses its protagonist's fatal illness to effect a revision of conventional perspectives. There sexual identity emerges as another discardable garment or role. First, she takes off 'for the last time the wrappings in which the world had known her' (*EC* 276). Next she discards her maternal life-role which now, like her 'womanly reserve[,] dropped like a rent veil'. What remains is death, and her soul 'aloof, proud, chill'. The rest is illusion:

> Now, the many happenings that composed it [her life] struck no answering chord in her; and it passed belief to think that she had once been stirred to the depths of her soul by them. In this hour of profounder knowledge, she

> saw that they had only been dreams and shadows — delusive images that had tricked her brain. Nothing of them had persisted; nothing been real or lasting: her hand had caught the frayed edge of no perdurable garment. … their hold upon her had been an imaginary one: her inmost self, the vitalest part of her, had remained unmoved by them, and unharmed. (*EC* 284)

Acknowledging yet transcending the most gruesome human suffering, this spiritualist-inspired tale recalls Olga Roncoroni's perception of Richardson as 'the least materialistic' of persons;[12] while its words, which render death a gateway rather than a fearful termination, anticipate the ending of *The Fortunes of Richard Mahony*: beside the corpse the night-light 'threw living shadows on the wall'.

In this story, the earthly garments from which the soul must free itself are specifically identified with the 'veil' of 'womanly reserve' — a figure developed oppressively in 'The Coat'. There Katherine, before going to meet her unmarried friend Margaret, seeks to hide her shabby, unhappily married state under a fur. It is supposedly the gift of a generous husband, but was actually bought with money stolen from his meagre savings. When the story opens Katherine is immersed like a Neoplatonic soul in the dictates of gender and materiality, weighed down by a coat of deceit and false identity intended to keep in place the romantic myths to which she has so fatally subscribed: 'she stood, the coat clinging and dragging like the water-logged clothes on a drowning man'. These, or rather their signifier the coat, later impede her in a 'jump for her life', so that she is hit by a passing bus. Before death and still encumbered by the coat, she reviews her existence, only to recognise damningly that she does not 'know any more what's true and what isn't' (*S* 60). The individual disclosed during her coma is one who endeavours to reject her origins and to deny her true motivation, and so cannot even begin the reforms which depend ultimately on personal resolve, not external norms, for as one spirit admonishes her: 'No one can help you but yourself, child. But be quick, your chance is passing' (*S* 59). Beneath the coat of enculturation there is, however, as little independent identity as in Paulchen, and a casualty ward scene externalises this through her now coat-free form, which is still 'monstrously distorted' and heavily bandaged. Finally, the focus shifts to a surrogate reader in Margaret who, 'deeply pitying, believed she understood', in a tantalising closure which thrusts the onus for interpretation and action back on the audience outside the narrative.

The sequence of stories entitled 'Growing Pains: Sketches of Girlhood' attempts to dissect the processes of socialisation which weave the veil or coat of conventional womanhood, and reflects gender issues which became prominent in European literature during the decades surrounding the Great War. This was a period which, according to Virginia Woolf, was without parallel for being 'so stridently sex-conscious', and Richardson herself claimed to have 'read Freud & his works so early in life — before his *name* was even known in England — that his theories have become a commonplace to me'.[13] Thanks to the Viennese psychoanalyst, and to other pioneer writers on sexuality such as Havelock Ellis, the Australian was heir to the post-Freudian notion of life diversely affected by the dictates of sexuality, and of gender as a mutable, social formation rather than a purely biological given. Her most productive years also coincided with renewed debate on sexual divergence, and with endeavours to repress or regulate it, or to render it invisible. The last applied particularly to a subject which interested Richardson: lesbianism. The notorious Labouchère Amendment to the Criminal Law Amendment Act of 1885, which made male homosexual acts illegal, failed to extend the same recognition to reciprocal female desire. Lesbianism was regarded at the time as being virtually non-existent as well as altogether too repellent. And the latter attitude still dominated parliamentary debate in 1921, when it was suggested that lesbian acts be included under the Labouchère Amendment: '"To adopt a clause of this kind", one MP proclaimed, "would harm by introducing into the minds of perfectly innocent people the most revolting thoughts"'.[14] The stories in 'Growing Pains' reveal a far more complex understanding of sexual motivation, and afford a distinctive contribution to the widespread contemporary questioning of received notions of masculine and feminine identity.

Richardson's targets in 'Growing Pains' are not new, though their mode of presentation is. Through different but psychologically related protagonists she focuses on the crucial phase which marks the awakening and shaping of female sexuality in an aggressively heterosexual culture. The girl of the opening tale is strikingly prepubescent:

> Stripped of her clothing, the child showed the lovely shape of a six-year-old. Just past the dimpled roundnesses of babyhood, the little body stood slim and straight, legs and knees closely met, the skin white as the sand into which the small feet dug, pink toe faultlessly matched to toe. (*EC* 71)

Her body is ready to receive its first engendering imprint. The sequence closes with physically mature women on the threshold of sexual experience, ending either with the female lovers of 'Two Hanged Women' or with a household of women anxiously awaiting a marriageable male in 'Sister Ann'. Largely invisible in the stories, although informing the experience of each female, is a patriarchal order which treats women exclusively as biologically determined sexual partners and mothers, and views their life, stripped of decorous subterfuge, as a necessary striving after their ordained fulfilment in marriage: 'Consequently young girls secretly regard their domestic or professional concerns as being of subsidiary importance, even as mere diversions. They consider their sole and serious calling love, conquests, and every thing related to them: their self-presentation, dancing, etc.'[15] Richardson's explorations of adolescent identity challenge dominant male versions of female reality. Women's common experience is stressed rather than their rivalry, their autonomous identity rather than their interchangeability, dependence or passivity, and their capacity for libidinous feelings independent of the opposite sex. Their vulnerability is shown to be not simply a natural given, but the result of unrelenting economies of surveillance and control which ensure the sway of seemingly self-evident gender codes.

The first two stories, 'The Bathe' and 'Three in a Row', are concerned with female self-imaging. This theme emerges explicitly in the closing meditation of Tetta, who, having escaped the confines of her assigned sleeping quarters, is on the point of falling asleep under the stars:

> And then something else came into her head — a familiar thought, and one she often amused herself with. It had to do with her own identity. Did there, she was given to wondering, somewhere or anywhere on earth exist a replica of herself? Was there, hidden away in some corner of the globe, another girl called Tetta Riley, thirteen years old, with a stub nose with freckles on it, and all her other little funniosities, who had grown up as she grew up, and who felt and thought like her? Herself, finding it hard to believe in her own uniqueness, she was inclined to think there might, there must be; and when, as now, she had nothing better to do, she would send her mind round the world in a fanciful search after her second self. To-night, in face of this starry splendour, she let it stray to what she believed to be 'other worlds', as well, chasing her thought among the stars and planets of the Milky Way. (*EC* 91)

The passage plays on the familiar 'other worlds' topos of Enlightenment literature, which undercut claims for earth's special position, and mediated a sense of greater, controlling forces beyond our sovereign will. Tetta, like the other protagonists, is in search of her own identity, but is unable to imagine it other than in known terms. Although the individual may wish to believe in her or his uniqueness, conditioning stresses the contrary, and informs our vision of creation from the particular instance to the nebulous stars on high. Certainly there is always escape into sleep; but even this is presented as having 'gathered her too into the fold' or group identity, and the rude awakenings portrayed in other tales suggest that Tetta's peaceful, self-willed quest is the dream, whereas reality compels the recognition of a shared female predicament.

This common lot is underscored by the opening tale, 'The Bathe', with its key motif of reflection. Just as the sea can mirror the land, so the unnamed six-year-old sees her future reflected in the socially inscribed bodies of two older women who survey her. Initially she frolics in the sea, clothed only in the natural element which is described as a second skin or cleansing veil, beyond the constraints of land. There the sexually mature women are located, and their decision to undress is presented as the release of accumulated sexual impulses, with clothing serving to figure graphically the constrictions that await the child:

> Tight stiff corsets were next squeezed from their moorings and cast aside … and stockings, their feet emerging red and tired-looking, the toes misshapen, and horny with callosities. Erect again, they yet coyly hesitated before casting off the last veil, once more sweeping the distance for a possible spy. (*EC* 73)

The action is at once a figurative putting out to sea and a reaffirmation of their suppressed identities, while their bondage is linked with an invisible but omnipresent male gaze. Richardson, 'who all her life had resolutely refused to wear corsets, or indeed any kind of clothing which might impede her movements',[16] elevates the feminist case for rational dress into an implicit arraignment of practices which reduce woman to a marketable commodity and misshape her natural self. Significantly, the child, who has never witnessed such a disrobing because she is usually asleep, flees in horror: 'suddenly she turned tail and ran back to the pool. She didn't want to see.' To her it is every bit as ominous as the bloody scene of parturition which shocks Ellen in *The Fortunes of Richard Mahony*. The vignette closes with the three returned to the beach. The women are strongly identified with child-bearing ('their contours were those of seals — great mother-seals come lolloping out of the water to lie about on the sand' (*EC* 76)); the girl with its rejection when she takes 'a piece of dry cuttlefish', an uncompromisingly infertile object, as plaything. Like Blake's heroine in *The Book of Thel*, the child is allowed to view the world of experience and to recoil from it; except that whereas Thel desires but acts not, Richardson's child seems denied future agency in a world where the procedures for regulating her biological progress are already firmly in place.

These images of reflection introduce a concern with female narcissism and autonomy. Narcissism, like the notion of phallocentrism, enters the parlance of modern psychoanalysis through the theories of Freud, which stress the formation of individual identity through the internalisation of diverse, libidinously invested images. In a woman this can involve identification with conventional female roles, such as motherhood, or envisaging herself as an object of desire, as in many *fin de siècle* tableaux of women who kiss their images in mirrors, or gaze entranced at their own reflection in water. Fulfilment, however, requires a phallus, without which Freud views her as an impoverished or incomplete being. But when a mirror is held up to Richardson's six-year-old she is greeted by a demystified image of the 'fruits' of phallic dominion:

> Above their knees, garters had cut fierce red lines in the skin; their bodies were criss-crossed with red furrows, from the variety of strings and bones that had lashed them in. The calves of one showed purple-knotted with veins; across the other's abdomen ran a deep, longitudinal scar. One was patched with red hair, one with black. (*EC* 74)

This catalogue of the horrors attendant on mature female sexuality is endorsed elsewhere by a young girl's recoil before rampant male sexuality, which 'rudely shatter[ed] their frail young dreams' (*EC* 123), or by another's loathing at the thought of a male embrace.

In a subsequent tale, 'The Bath', the opening seascape shrinks to a zinc tub 'streaked rust-brown from the tidemarks of the many waters that had filled it' (*EC* 112), though Richardson's critique of enculturation remains unchanged. Here young girls play again, unconscious of the nearby clock and mirror which embody the immutable passage of biological time and the reflection this engenders. 'Clothed, it was otherwise.' Unfettered innocence disappears with the donning of social signifiers, of which prescribed femineity is another 'garment' imposed on each primal identity. Yet the author remains aware of the naked or particularised entity that exists beneath the surface. Hence she appropriates the traditional mirror metaphor of realist art, not to underscore narcissism or, as in the case of Stendhal and Flaubert, an artistic project concerned with reflecting back life's multiplicity, but as a means of conjuring up hidden, and otherwise proscribed, depths:

> Four times the door opened and shut; till the room was empty. The splashed walls and swimming floor drained dry; the bath-water gurgled off; and the mirror's surface lay blank, no conjurer being at hand to call to life the lovely shapes that slumbered in its depth. (*EC* 116)

The unknown depths, identified by Freud with the unconscious, are recast as the suppressed and secret identity of womankind. Denied its own sphere and autonomous expression by male authority, its recuperation becomes the resisting woman writer's task — the aim of her art to people the apparent emptiness and to make the silence speak.[17]

Viewed collectively, the stories of 'Growing Pains' shift from scenes of enclosure to enlarged prospects as the protagonists mature, but in ways which interrogate the stereotypes that such a progress normally underwrites. According to romantic and philosophic saws, maturation is accompanied by increased self-knowledge and mastery. These culminate in the ultimate release of marriage, when woman moves from the subordination of girlhood to an independent and fulfilling sphere. This paradigm, as Richardson subtly shows, bears little resemblance to actualities. The charmed tidal pool of childhood in the first tale gives way in succession to bedroom, hayloft and pantry — all sites either assigned to young womanhood or chosen as places of privacy away from the demands of the adult world. Yet this sense of refuge is delusory, as even these spaces have been invaded by outside codes. In 'Three in a Row' the girls have already been inculcated with a sense of duty, propriety and beauty, but are still drawn to a realm without bounds — a dimension whose virtual disappearance coincides with the intrusive presence of sexuality. In the next story, the stars and limitless possibilities which enthralled Tetta have dwindled to the false diamonds on a hair-slide, and to the sexual resonances of hair and exposure. These the clip is vainly intended to control, whereas nascent libidinal impulses dictate that Peggy's play with Rex, when 'short skirts fluttered and ballooned', is only a 'preliminary canter'.

Repeatedly the stories underline that maturation brings necessarily neither crucial knowledge nor empowerment. Even for the seventeen-year-old of 'A Conversation in a Pantry', sex remains 'the great unknown', a tantalising yet constraining mystery telescoped into the rooms of sleeping couples which the adolescent girls pass on their way to and from the pantry. There they find tartlets for a midnight snack. But their female bonding and self-sufficiency are soon undermined by Alice's longings for her boyfriend, leading Trixie to ponder despairingly: 'Oh, *why* are men and women, Dallie? Why have they got to be?' (*EC* 109). The female moon, which 'hung like a round cheese in the sky' and blessed their enterprise, has by story's end 'shrunk to the size of a pippin', and a realm of bright possibility been dimmed by a disturbing future, associated with male snores which to Trix assume a 'strange and sinister significance'.

Increasingly as 'Growing Pains' unfolds, untroubled 'lovely shapes' are displaced by disconcerting images of women's fate as Richardson uses the magical mirror of art to reveal dashed heterosexual dreams. A keynote is struck with the title 'The Wrong Turning', for each of her ensuing female protagonists finishes by finding her experience at odds with the authorised version of gender relations. This tale focuses on the gap that separates romantic dreams and sublimations from coarse reality. The adolescent heroine, casting aside the demeaning signs of her schoolgirl state, projects herself into the fantasy of a romantic outing, propelled by a strong, oar-wielding youth. Both are soon lost in their preferred reveries, the individual companion quickly fading into a generic type: 'Oh, it was a fine thing to be able to row so well, and have a girl, *the* girl, sitting watching you. For now her eyes hung on him, mutely adoring, spurring him on to ever bolder strokes' (*EC* 120–1). A mistaken branch of the river and missing palings in a fence, designed to keep from view naked male swimmers, provide a sudden revelation of forces underlying their imaginings which disconcert both dreamers: 'breaking down his boyish privacy, pitching her headlong into a reality for which she was in no wise prepared' (*EC* 123). It is a similar rude awakening to that experienced by Dolly in 'And Women

Must Weep'. Here the recurrent mirror motif reflects not hidden depths, but social valuations. Dolly as debutante is togged out to befit her name, and to produce a desirable object. Dancing, so glibly enumerated by male commentators among the standard female arts, is revealed to be yet another arena of potential ordeal, where woman, no less than during a boating party, is dependent on male initiative and good will. The evening becomes an exercise in personal humiliation, a prescribed showing and offering of the self to an ungraciously uninterested public. If at the outset Dolly 'hardly recognised herself in the glass' because of her new finery, at the end this is doubly so given the enforced rereading of her attire and her growing self-consciousness. For the story closes with a young woman in full rebellion against heterosexual norms. Not only does she rail against 'these men, who walked round and chose just who they fancied and left who they didn't' (*EC* 130), but she recognises that 'she hadn't wanted "the gentlemen" any more than they'd wanted her: she had only had to pretend to' (*EC* 132–3).

This sense of injustice and repulsion at the proffered male norm of sexuality culminates in 'Two Hanged Women'. Its themes and preoccupations foreground the current of dissent implicit in previous stories, and complement especially those of 'The Bathe'. There the young innocent moved instinctively further away from the land with its terrifying marks of inscribed gender codes. The final tale portrays two mutually attracted women, who are similarly driven out beyond the safe, public areas by heterosexual derision and incomprehension. Their ensuing exchange on the breakwater reveals the conflicting pressures to which the younger and sexually undecided girl is subjected. Unrelenting social coercion is counterbalanced by an aversion to physical intimacy with the opposite sex which, in her eyes, becomes a fearful grotesque: 'And if he tries to touch me, Betty, or even takes my arm or puts his round me. … And then his face … when it looks like it does sometimes … all wrong … as if it had gone all wrong — oh! then I feel I shall have to scream — out loud' (140). This confession reverses the standard perspective, and lends particularity to a fear that has haunted various female watchers from the six-year-old and Nellie to the adolescent distressed after the boat-trip, who ran away 'as if chased by some grotesque nightmare-shape which she must leave far, far behind her ... even in thought' (*EC* 123). Far from being odd or queer, as society would label it, the reaction of Betty is the culmination of recurring responses which problematise the apparently natural sway of heterosexuality, and highlight the play of communal forces in the formation of gender and sexual preference.

The final phase of Richardson's counter-case, withheld until the concluding paragraph, moves beyond criticism to offer a re-envisaged emblem of female love. In place of a mother enforcing the phallic code, or the tableau of seal-like women cumbersomely regaining the land in 'The Bathe', 'Two Hanged Women' ends by identifying lesbian longing with all that is best in maternal care and passion:

> But at this last appeal she [Betty] melted; and gathering the young girl to her breast, she held her fast. — And so for long she continued to sit, her chin resting lightly on the fair hair, that was silky and downy as an infant's, and gazing with sombre eyes over the stealthily heaving sea. (*EC* 141)

The grip is protective not possessive, the love reciprocal and unforced, and the situation one where physical contact conjures up untainted fulfilment rather than grotesque nightmares.

With time a more cautious Richardson decided to end her fine sequence with the less openly transgressive story 'Sister Ann'. Its basic story-line deals with the need to find suitable mates for the six marriageable O'Grady daughters. This conventionally heterosexual plot is complicated by the seventh and eldest daughter's assumption of the parental role of facilitator of social encounters for her siblings, and by its interweaving with selected motifs from the Bluebeard legend. The story opens with a well-known literary quotation which is immediately contextualised:

> 'Sister Ann, Sister Ann, do you see anyone coming?' — from cowering Fatima. And from the look-out always the monotonous reply: 'Naught but the dust that blows before the wind!'
>
> She was really Edith; but ever since as children they had acted the Bluebeard play, she had been *ANN* to them — Sister Ann. And the name fitted her. For Ann quite literally spent her life on the watch for the next disaster, she being the only one who might possibly ward it off. (*S* 21)

Edith is, and is not, Sister Ann, and this potential duality will be exploited in her climactic decision-making. 'Nearing forty' herself, she has written off her own marital prospects in favour of furthering those of her sisters, though all her plans have been frustrated until that 'unicum', a wealthy middle-aged bachelor, is introduced into their midst. She proceeds to offer him her most attractive siblings, but is nonplussed when his choice falls on her. Her initial refusal of his hand, however, provides the occasion for her sisters to hold up to her a shocking, because strongly critical, version of her domestic role. Benignly intended actions are reread as enslaving and tyrannical. The resulting cruel 'wound to her self-love' distances her sufficiently from them to enable her to envisage matrimony as an acceptable alternative, and as a more effective means of helping her family. Sister Ann has to be dispelled in part by Edith, and the tale concludes with her sisters also freed to follow their suppressed impulses, including the beautiful Gemma, who is found meditating on 'how, without loss of dignity, to lure back the tall, dark, handsome lover so boorishly shown the door by Sister Ann' (*S* 32).

The unspoken problem raised for the reader by this familiar comedy of manners is what or where is Bluebeard in all this. In Charles Perrault's original tale *La Barbe bleue* (1697), Bluebeard leaves his seventh and newly married wife in charge of his castle. During his absence she enters a forbidden room and discovers there the corpses of his former wives. Threatened with decapitation as punishment for her disobedience, she bids her sister mount a tower in search of deliverance, and asks the pathetic question which opens Richardson's story. In Grimm's *Hausmärchen* three sisters are similarly threatened, one of whom saves the other two, and both versions end with the timely, cavalry-like arrival of their brothers. 'Sister Ann' apparently dispenses with Bluebeard, the locked room, dangerous female curiosity and eleventh-hour rescue. Or does it? Rather the elemental threat to womankind assumes a number of shifting forms. Most obviously, it is the imperative to marry, driven by the menacing opprobrium of a spinster's title. Next, the role is arguably assumed by Pa O'Grady, whose neglect of his daughters' primal need constitutes incarceration on an isolated property, and a virtual death sentence. Finally, Ann unexpectedly emerges as a major force blocking their individual fulfilment in her role as surrogate patriarch and plotting tyrant; yet she also assumes the role of the seventh wife whose actions break the cycle of female imprisonment and untimely death. As such Ann has both to overcome and be true to herself. This Richardson achieves by giving her a suitor who releases her from a dominant role over the siblings, and who especially admires her practical and managerial qualities. The original's negative view of female motivation and curiosity is here elided in favour of a realistic appraisal of female desire and an awareness that even six, similarly placed sisters are clearly autonomous entities, ranging from languid Gemma to Ann for 'whom work's a sort of gospel'. The melodrama of Perrault's tale yields to a romantic resolution, but one which implicitly attacks existing conditions that reduce womankind to the opening archetype of 'cowering Fatima',[18] and shows male–female bonding to be more complex and varied than conventional formulae allow.

As her tales and novels amply demonstrated, Richardson was neither passive in the face of history, nor Paulchen-like in her self-absorption. Instead, she could argue with equal conviction that it was imperative to kill Fascists,[19] or for the need to re-envisage women's social role and individual identity. Whereas conventional wisdom asserted that 'all women can do is to reproduce what someone else has thought or felt' (*MG* 61), she recast the topoi of romantic love, school-day and settler experience, and adolescent maturation to highlight their traditional blindnesses and the special dilemmas faced by her sex. Similarly, much as she admired Jacobsen, she could not accept the pessimistic quietism which informs his detached analysis of characters such as Niels Lyhne's mother: 'she dreamed a thousand dreams of those sunny places and was consumed with longing for her true, rich self, forgetting what it is so easy to forget, that even the fairest dreams, even the deepest longings, add not a single inch to the stature of the human soul'.[20] Eschewing defeatism, Richardson contested the limiting stereotypes foisted on women, while adopting an intellectual position closer to that of 'old Goethe', for whom she confessed to having 'a great liking'.[21] For in her words it was 'he who "saw life steadily & saw it whole"', and who enacted, no less than herself, Faust's doctrine of eternal self-making:

> Ja! diesem Sinne bin ich ganz ergeben,
> Das ist der Weisheit letzter Schluß:
> Nur der verdient sich Freiheit wie das Leben,

Der täglich sie erobern muß.

(Yes, I am completely committed to this,
Which is wisdom's final conclusion:
Only he earns freedom, like life,
Who daily has to conquer it.)[22]

In her case, seeing life whole entailed exploring the last 'dark continent' designated by Freud, that of uncharted women's experience, as well as confronting the Nietzschean seven devils of the individual creator. The result was a sombre past transmuted into enduring art, and life-knowledge refashioned not merely into self-involved texts, but into universal paradigms, which align her ultimately among both nationalist authors and seminal contributors to the women's movement.

NOTES

1 THE SECRET SELF

1 See Dorothy Green, *Henry Handel Richardson and Her Fiction* (Angus & Robertson, Sydney, 1986), 582. Hereafter referred to as *Richardson.*
2 Richardson, *Myself When Young* (Heinemann, London, 1948), 126.
3 Richardson, 'Some Notes on my Books', *Southerly*, 23 (1963), 14.
4 *Richardson*, 572.
5 Edna Purdie and Olga M. Roncoroni (eds), *Henry Handel Richardson: Some Personal Impressions* (Angus & Robertson, Sydney, 1957), 103. Hereafter referred to as *Impressions.*
6 This transition, however, was not clear cut. Axel Clark reports that Ettie was still composing original music and fiction in Munich in 1896 (*Henry Handel Richardson: Fiction in the Making* (Simon & Schuster, Sydney, 1990), 235–6).
7 Richardson, 'A Danish Poet', *Southerly*, 23 (1963), 43.
8 ibid., 46–7.
9 *Siren Voices (Niels Lyhne)*, trans. Ethel F. L. Robertson (Heinemann, London, 1896), 3.
10 ibid., 3–4.
11 ibid., 3.
12 Letter of Mary Kernot to Richardson, 22 March 1931, ML MSS 325. (ML indicates a manuscript collection held at the Mitchell Library, Sydney.)
13 *Impressions*, 74.
14 *Richardson*, 177.
15 Letter of Mary Kernot to Richardson, 15 June 1912, ML MSS 325. Their correspondence for this year canvasses a number of key feminist issues.
16 *Impressions*, 48.
17 Letter to Oliver Stonor, 3 October 1938, ML MSS 546.
18 The phrase appears in 'A Danish Poet', 50.
19 Alex Owen, *The Darkened Room: Women, Power and Spiritualism in Late Victorian England* (University of Pennyslvania Press, Philadelphia, 1990), 11.

20 *Impressions*, 77. Roncoroni emphasises the scientific and research aspects of these memberships, as distinct from the interests of others who willingly let themselves be imposed on by charlatan clairvoyants and fraudulent practices.
21 Letter to Oliver Stonor, 13 January n.d. (1932?), ML MSS 546.
22 *Richardson*, 16.
23 Note dated 19 July 1918, repr. in *Impressions*, 82–3.
24 Note dated 28 May 1933, repr. in *Impressions*, 103.
25 Letter to Oliver Stonor, 17 June 1940, ML MSS 546.
26 ibid., 29 April 1941.
27 From Zweig, *The World of Yesterday* (Cassell, London, 1943), 77; repr. in Elaine Showalter, *Sexual Anarchy: Gender and Culture in the Fin de Siècle* (Bloomsbury Publishing, London, 1991), 196.
28 Cited in *Sexual Anarchy*, 197.
29 *Richardson*, 587. Green also mentions here the possible infection of Richardson's mother.
30 Richardson herself had no progeny, explaining this credibly but perhaps disingenuously as a vocation for which other women were better suited.
31 As Clark notes in *Henry Handel Richardson: Fiction in the Making*, the cause of her father's general paralysis 'remained a mystery until 1913 when Noguchi and Moore established that it was a tertiary stage of syphilis' (105).
32 *Richardson*, 567.
33 Philip Mead, 'Death and Home-work: The Origins of Narrative in *The Fortunes of Richard Mahony*', *Australian Literary Studies*, 17 (1995), 120.
34 *Impressions*, 106.
35 Nietzsche, *Werke*, ed. Karl Schlechta (Ullstein Verlag, Frankfurt/M, 1969), II, 601. All translations from the German are my own. Richardson's intimate acquaintance with Nietzsche's ideas cannot be doubted. Not only do her diaries attest to serious engagement with his works, but years later she could refer to him as 'a writer of the most exquisite prose that has ever come from any German pen' (Letter to Oliver Stonor, 20 April 1942, ML MSS 546).
36 Undated note, perhaps a translation or random thought, Richardson Papers, NL MSS 133. (NL indicates a manuscript collection held at the National Library, Canberra.)
37 Respectively *Impressions*, 136, and letter to Mrs Ransen, 25 February 1935, ML MSS 287.
38 Letter to Richardson, 3 March 1939, ML MSS 325.
39 'A Danish Poet', 42.

2 DECENTRING THE KÜNSTLERROMAN

1 This copy is held in the Richardson Papers, NL MSS 133. 'Nub' is an affectionate name for her husband.
2 ibid., 38.
3 ibid., 46.
4 *Myself When Young*, 166.
5 Erich Trunz (ed.), *Goethes Werke* (Beck, München, 1973), VII, 431.
6 *Myself When Young*, 154.
7 'Henry Handel Richardson's *Maurice Guest*', *Meanjin*, 2 (1955), 186–99; repr. in Clement Semmler (ed.), *Twentieth Century Australian Literary Criticism* (Oxford University Press, Melbourne, 1967), 295–309.
8 *Richardson*, 161–88.
9 Undated note, Richardson Papers, NL MSS 133.
10 *Richardson*, 587.
11 Weininger, *Geschlecht und Charakter: eine prinzipielle Untersuchung* (Wilhelm Braumüller, Wien, 1903), 413.
12 Jacques le Ridet, *Der Fall Otto Weininger: Wurzeln des Antifeminismus und Antisemitismus* (Löcker Verlag, Wien, 1985), 221.
13 Weininger, *Über die letzten Dinge* (Wilhelm Braumüller, Wien, 1922), 59–60.
14 ibid., 60.
15 *Geschlecht und Charakter*, 116.
16 ibid., 277. Pope's judgement is uttered in 'Epistle to a Lady: Of the Characters of Women' (1735), l. 270.
17 Cited in Ridet, *Der Fall Otto Weininger*, 52.
18 This and subsequent views are drawn from 'Über die Weiber' ('About Women'), ch. 27 in *Parerga und Paralipomena.*
19 *Geschlecht und Charakter*, 321–2.
20 Letter to Oliver Stonor, 23 September 1939, ML MSS 546.
21 Nietzsche, *Werke*, II, 604.
22 *Myself When Young*, 125.
23 'A Danish Poet', 47.
24 *Siren Voices (Niels Lyhne)*, 90–1.
25 *Geschlecht und Charakter*, 324.
26 *Siren Voices (Niels Lyhne)*, 218.
27 ibid., 198–9.
28 *Erdgeist* (Goldmann Verlag, München, 1970), 15.
29 *The Flame*, trans. Susan Bassnett (Quartet Books, London, 1991), 106.
30 ibid., 112.
31 Letter to Miss Ransen, 25 February 1935, ML MSS 287.

32 Letter to Oliver Stonor, 28 October 1939, ML MSS 546.
33 'Some Notes on my Books', 12.

3 FIGURES OF SUBVERSION

1 *A History of German Literature*, rev. edn (Blackwood, Edinburgh, 1949), 441.
2 Letter to Oliver Stonor, 29 April 1941, ML MSS 546.
3 *Impressions*, 152.
4 Richardson confesses as much in *Myself When Young*, 24.
5 In context this refers to his entire dependence on inspiration rather than mechanical means of composition, but the link with the wider issue of life-experience is implicit.
6 Commentary has focused primarily on this aspect of his influence, following the account of her encounter with Hoffmann's portrayal of a high musical calling given in *Myself When Young*, 77–8.
7 E. T. A. Hoffmann, *Sämtliche poetischen Werke* (Tempel Verlag, Berlin, 1963), II, 163.
8 Hoffmann, *Sämtliche poetischen Werke*, I, 632.
9 Although Richardson felt bound to stay close to received accounts of the Wagner circle, and in fact consulted a formidable range of secondary material (see her bibliography, *YC* 339–40), she still had freedom to choose specific periods and incidents for fictionalisation.
10 Ivo Frenzel, *Friedrich Nietzsche in Selbstzeugnissen und Bilddokumenten* (Rowohlt Verlag, Reinbek bei Hamburg, 1966), 134.
11 See letters to Oliver Stonor of 3 and 18 May 1939, ML MSS 546.
12 Schopenhauer, 'Über die Weiber', *Sämtliche Werke*, ed. Wolfgang von Löhneysen (Wissenschaftliche Buchgesellschaft, Darmstadt, 1965), V, 726–7.
13 The penultimate line contains an implicit rejection of the naturalistic mode of *A Doll's House*, where Nora delights in playing with her children and in the forbidden eating of macaroons.
14 Aeschylus, *The Oresteian Trilogy*, trans. Philip Vellacott (Penguin, Harmondsworth, 1971), 86. In its original context the phrase embraces womankind, despite even outward manifestations of individual power and authority.
15 'Some Notes on my Books', 13.
16 These are listed in full, together with their locations and translations, in Karen McLeod, *Henry Handel Richardson: A Critical Study* (Cambridge University Press, Cambridge, 1985), 244–5.
17 'Vom höheren Menschen', *Werke*, II, 798–800.
18 ibid., 802.
19 'Some Notes on my Books', 12.

20 *Werke*, II, 797–8.
21 ibid., 803.
22 As Jean Templeton remarks, 'to read the [last] scene is to meet a compendium of everything that early modern feminism denounced about women's state' ('The *Doll House* Backlash: Criticism, Feminism, and Ibsen', *PMLA*, 104 (1989), 32).
23 *Werke*, II, 803–4.
24 'The Nostalgia of Permanence and the Fiend of Motion' in *Henry Handel Richardson 1870–1946: Papers Presented at a Centenary Seminar* (National Library, Canberra, 1972), 57.
25 Richardson's abiding view of the Germans was that 'they are musical to the finger-tips (or were)' (Letter to Oliver Stonor, 2 October 1939, ML MSS 546).
26 See respectively 'The Story of Wagner and von Bülow — and the woman behind their music', *Southerly*, 23 (1963), 64, and letter to Oliver Stonor, 28 October 1939, ML MSS 546.
27 See respectively Joseph von Eichendorff's 'Wünschelrute': 'A song sleeps in all things / Which dream on and on / And the world begins to sing / If you once strike the magic word' (*Werke* (Winkler Verlag, München, 1970), I, 132), and Michael Ackland, *That Shining Band: A Study of Australian Colonial Verse Tradition* (University of Queensland Press, Brisbane, 1994), 3–9.
28 'Some Notes on my Books', 14 — a point of view reiterated by Robertson in 'The Art of Henry Handel Richardson' (*Myself When Young*, 179).
29 *Werke*, II, 601.

4 RE-ENVISAGING THE NATIONAL SCRIPT

1 *Richardson*, 568–9.
2 'A Danish Poet', 50.
3 On its formation and contents see Kay Schaffer, *Women and the Bush: Forces of Desire in the Australian Cultural Tradition* (Cambridge University Press, Melbourne, 1988).
4 See Ackland, *That Shining Band*, 20–37.
5 'The Art of Henry Handel Richardson', in *Myself When Young*, 206.
6 *Myself When Young*, 24.
7 See Elizabeth Lawson, '"A Rather Prosaic Wife", or The Fortunes of Mary Mahony', *Westerly*, 30 (1985), 76–8.
8 See the entries for March, April and August. All diaries referred to are held in the Richardson Papers, NL MSS 133.
9 Diary entry, April 1898. Richardson was also working intensely on Nietzsche at this time.
10 According to Green, 'a number of references to Schopenhauer have been expunged from the final typescript of *Maurice Guest*' (*Richardson*, 50). A full

appreciation of the effect of these changes must await the forthcoming variorum edition of the novel.

11 On his equally important disagreements with Kant see Bryan Magee, *The Philosophy of Schopenhauer* (Clarendon Press, Oxford, 1983), 96–9 and *passim*; and Christopher Janaway, *Self and World in Schopenhauer's Philosophy* (Clarendon Press, Oxford, 1989).

12 *Welt und Mensch: Eine Auswahl aus dem Gesamtwerk*, ed. Arthur Hübscher (Reclam, Stuttgart, 1966), 33–4. Wherever possible quotations of Schopenhauer's work are drawn from this readily available edition.

13 ibid., 34.

14 Schopenhauer, *Sämtliche Werke*, I, 37.

15 From *Die Geburt der Tragödie*, in *Werke*, I, 101.

16 Bertrand Russell, *A History of Western Philosophy* (Allen & Unwin, London, 1984), 724. For the passage quoted by Russell see *Welt und Mensch*, 30.

17 *Welt und Mensch*, 79.

18 Robertson, *A History of German Literature*, 472.

19 *Welt und Mensch*, 79.

20 ibid., 80.

21 ibid., 81.

22 ibid., 78.

23 *Moby-Dick*, ed. Harrison Hayford and Hershel Parker (Norton, New York, 1967), 347.

24 This decision, in Schopenhauer's terms, remains an expression or extension of our will-defined inadequacies and conceptions. The alternative form of negation is described in *Welt und Mensch*, 117–8.

5 PARABLES OF IDENTITY

1 This was still the case as recently as 1985, in the last book-length study of Richardson by Karen McLeod, although much has been done to redress this view by Carol Franklin's detailed discussions of individual tales.

2 Letter to Jacob Schwartz, 25 January 1932, ML MSS 1146. Individual stories were published intermittently between 1911 and 1949.

3 Undated note, Richardson Papers, NL MSS 133.

4 *Impressions*, 99.

5 Letters to Oliver Stonor of 23 September and 2 October 1939, ML MSS 546.

6 Letters to Oliver Stonor of 3 October 1938 and 17 September 1939, ML MSS 546.

7 Letter to Oliver Stonor, 19 December 1939, ML MSS 546.

8 'Unrat' is a play on words, suggesting both without counsel or idea and refuse.

9 *Der Untertan* (Deutscher Taschenbuch Verlag, Hamburg, 1964), 243.

10 ibid., 337. See this and the ensuing pages for a satiric summary of the place of women in Wilhelminian Germany.

11 ibid., 341.

12 *Impressions*, 106.

13 Woolf is cited in Sandra M. Gilbert and Susan Gubar, *The War of the Words* (Yale University Press, New Haven, 1987), 3; and letter to Oliver Stonor, 18 May 1939, ML MSS 546.

14 Cited in Showalter, *Sexual Anarchy*, 119.

15 From 'Über die Weiber', Schopenhauer, *Sämtliche Werke* , V, 721.

16 *Impressions*, 163.

17 See Judith Fetterley, *The Resisting Reader: A Feminist Approach to American Fiction* (Indiana University Press, Bloomington, 1978), for a discussion of the general concept, and Carol Franklin's articles listed in the Bibliography for its specific application to Richardson.

18 Fatima is the name of a famous site of pilgrimage identified with the Virgin Mary, as well as of the founder of a tragic line associated with the House of Mohammed. As such, the reference to 'cowering Fatima' evokes a helpless archetype and a religious tradition which enshrines virginity and female purity.

19 Letter to Oliver Stonor, 9 September 1939, which continues: 'And it wld give me an unholy joy to slit the gizzards of some of those fiendish monsters who have tortured innocent people — some of my personal friends among them' (ML MSS 546).

20 *Siren Voices (Niels Lyhne)*, 3.

21 Letter to Oliver Stonor, 29 April 1941, ML MSS 546.

22 *Goethes Werke*, III, 348.

BIBLIOGRAPHY

Duwell, Martin & Hergenhan, Laurie (eds), *The ALS Guide to Australian Literature: A Bibliography 1963–1990* (University of Queensland Press, Brisbane, 1992).

Howells, Gay (ed.), *Henry Handel Richardson: A Bibliography to honour the Centenary of her Birth* (National Library of Australia, Canberra, 1970).

Southerly, 23, 1 (1963) is a special issue devoted to Richardson which reprints most of her significant essays, and 'The Coat' and 'Sister Ann', two stories not contained in the 1934 collection of her shorter fiction.

PRINCIPAL WORKS BY HENRY HANDEL RICHARDSON

Books

Maurice Guest (Heinemann, London, 1908).

The Getting of Wisdom (Heinemann, London, 1910).

The Fortunes of Richard Mahony. Australia Felix. 1. (Heinemann, London, 1907).

The Way Home; being the second part of the chronicle of the fortunes of Richard Mahony (Heinemann, London, 1925).

Ultima Thule; being the third part of the chronicle of the fortunes of Richard Mahony (Heinemann, London, 1929).

The Fortunes of Richard Mahony; comprising Australia felix, The way home and Ultima Thule (Heinemann, London, 1930).

Two Studies (Ulysses Press, London, 1931).

The End of a Childhood and Other Stories (Heinemann, London, 1934).

The Young Cosima (Heinemann, London, 1939).

Myself When Young. Together with an Essay on The Art of Henry Handel Richardson by J. G. Robertson (Heinemann, London, 1948).

Translations

Jacobsen, J.P., *Siren Voices (Niels Lyhne)* (Heinemann, London, 1896).

Björnson, Björnstjerne, *The Fisher Lass* (Heinemann, London, 1896).

CRITICAL REFERENCES

Books

Buckley, Vincent, *Henry Handel Richardson* (Lansdowne, Melbourne, 1962; rev. edn Oxford University Press, Melbourne, 1970).

Clark, Axel, *Henry Handel Richardson: Fiction in the Making* (Simon & Schuster/New Endeavour, Sydney, 1990).

Corones, Eva Jarring, *The Portrayal of Women in the Fiction of Henry Handel Richardson* (Gleerup, Lund, 1983).

Douglas, Dennis, *Maurice Guest: Henry Handel Richardson* (Edward Arnold, Melbourne, 1978).

Elliott, William D., *Henry Handel Richardson: Ethel Florence Lindesay Richardson* (Twayne, Boston, 1975).

Green, Dorothy, *Ulysses Bound: Henry Handel Richardson and Her Fiction* (Australian National University Press, Canberra, 1973; rev. edn Allen & Unwin, Sydney, 1986).

Kramer, Leonie, *Henry Handel Richardson* (Oxford University Press, Melbourne, 1966).

—— *Myself When Laura: Fact and Fiction in Henry Handel Richardson's School Career* (Heinemann, Melbourne, 1966).

McLeod, Karen, *Henry Handel Richardson* (Cambridge University Press, Cambridge, 1985).

Odeen, Elizabeth, '*Maurice Guest*': *A Study* (University of Texas Press, Austin, 1964).

Purdie, Edna & Roncoroni, Olga M. (eds), *Henry Handel Richardson: Some Personal Impressions* (Angus & Robertson, Sydney, 1957).

Articles and Essays

Bennett, Jack W., 'The Frontier Legacy: Willa Cather and Henry Handel Richardson', *Antipodes*, 1 (1987), 35–9.

Bird, Delys, 'Towards an Aesthetic of Australian Women's Fiction: *My Brilliant Career* and *The Getting of Wisdom*', *Australian Literary Studies*, 9 (1984), 171–81.

Bock, Hanne K., 'Henry Handel Richardson: Letters to Brandes', *Southerly*, 43 (1983), 438–49.

Brady, Veronica, '"A Thick Crumbly Slice of Life": *The Fortunes of Richard Mahony* as a Cultural Monument', *Westerly*, 3 (1977), 47–56.

Butcher, Margaret K., 'From *Maurice Guest* to *Martha Quest*: The Female *Bildungsroman* in Commonwealth Literature', *World Literature Written in English*, 21 (1982), 254–62.

Clark, Dymphna, 'The Aurora Borealis: Henry Handel Richardson as a Translator', *Quadrant*, 17 (1973), 21–30.

Douglas, Dennis, 'H. H. Richardson: The Education of an Australian Realist', *Studies in the Novel*, 4 (1972), 141–53.

Foster, I.M., 'Richard Mahony's Tragedy', *Australian Literary Studies*, 4 (1970), 279–80.

Franklin, Carol, 'The Female *Künstlerroman*: Richardson *versus* Björnson', *Southerly*, 43 (1983), 422–36.

—— 'Mansfield and Richardson: A Short Story Dialectic', *Australian Literary Studies*, 11 (1983), 227–33.

—— 'The Not-so-objective-correlative. "Germany" in the Work of Four Antipodean Women Writers', *Kunapipi*, 12 (1990), 56–69.

—— 'The Resisting Writer: H. H. Richardson's Parody of Gogol', *AUMLA*, 68 (1987), 233–50.

—— Introduction to *The End of a Childhood: The complete Stories of Henry Handel Richardson* (Angus & Robertson, Sydney, 1992), v–xv.

Green, Dorothy, 'The Pilgrim Soul: The Philosophical Structure of *The Fortunes of Richard Mahony*', *Meanjin*, 28 (1969), 328–37.

—— 'Power-Games in the Novels of Henry Handel Richardson', in Shirley Walker (ed.), *Who is She?* (University of Queensland Press, Brisbane, 1983), 84–97.

—— 'The Nostalgia of Permanence and the Fiend of Motion', in *Henry Handel Richardson 1870–1946: Papers Presented at a Centenary Seminar* (National Library of Australia, Canberra, 1972), 48–62.

—— 'The Tradition of Social Responsibility in the Australian Novel: Richardson and Furphy', *Literary Criterion*, 15 (1980), 23–34.

—— 'Walter Lindesay Richardson: The Man, the Portrait, and the Artist', *Meanjin*, 29 (1970), 5–20.

—— '*The Young Cosima*', *Australian Literary Studies*, 4 (1970), 215–26.

Kiernan, Brian, 'The Fortunes of Richard Mahony', *Southerly*, 29 (1969), 199–209.

—— 'Romantic Conventions and *Maurice Guest*', *Southerly*, 28 (1968), 286–94.

Kramer, Leonie, 'Henry Handel Richardson', in Geoffrey Dutton (ed.), *The Literature of Australia* (Penguin, Ringwood, 1964), 318–31.

Loder, Elizabeth, 'The Fortunes of Richard Mahony: Dream and Nightmare', *Southerly*, 25 (1965), 251–63.

—— '*Maurice Guest*: Some Nineteenth-Century Progenitors', *Southerly*, 26 (1966), 94–105.

Macainsh, Noel, 'Point-of-View and Consequent Naturalism in the Novels of Henry Handel Richardson', *Westerly*, 29 (1984), 61–70.

—— 'The Shock of Recognition: Henry Handel Richardson and J. P. Jacobsen's *Niels Lyhne*', *Southerly*, 36 (1976), 99–111.

McFarlane, Brian, '*The Getting of Wisdom*: Not "Merry" At All', *Australian Literary Studies*, 8 (1977), 51–63.
—— 'Power in Dark Places: *The Fortunes of Richard Mahony*', *Southerly*, 37 (1977), 211–28.
Mann, Maureen C., 'The Genesis of *The Young Cosima*: Henry Handel Richardson's most Neglected Novel', *World Literature Written in English*, 17 (1978), 96–105.
Mead, Philip, 'Death and Home-work: The Origins of Narrative in *The Fortunes of Richard Mahony*', *Australian Literary Studies*, 17 (1995), 115–34.
Palmer, Anthony J., 'A Link with Late Nineteenth-Century Decadence in *Maurice Guest*', *Australian Literary Studies*, 5 (1972), 366–73.
Pratt, Catherine, 'Fictions of Development: Henry Handel Richardson's *The Getting of Wisdom*', *Antipodes*, 9 (1995), 3–9.
Stewart, Ken, '*The Fortunes of Richard Mahony*: Symphony and Naturalism', in W. S. Ramson (ed.), *The Australian Experience: Critical Essays on Australian Novels* (Australian National University Press, Canberra, 1974), 97–120.
—— '*Maurice Guest* and the Siren Voices', *Australian Literary Studies*, 5 (1972), 352–65.
—— 'The Prototype of Richard Mahony', *Australian Literary Studies*, 4 (1970), 227–40.
Thomson, A.K., 'Henry Handel Richardson's *The Fortunes of Richard Mahony*', *Meanjin*, 26 (1967), 423–34.
Wattie, Nelson, 'Henry Handel Richardson and the German *Bildungsroman*', *Commonwealth*, 6 (1984), 22–8.
Wilkes, G.A., 'Henry Handel Richardson: Some Associations', *Southerly*, 47 (1987), 207–13.
Zwicky, Fay, 'Maurice the Obscure: Provincial Expatriate in Search of a Voice', *Meridian*, 4 (1985), 99–111.

Acknowledgements

I am very grateful to the National Library and the Mitchell Library for the splendid access and conditions they provided, which made working on their manuscript collections a pleasure. I would also like to thank Chris Wallace-Crabbe for his encouragement with this project, and for his perceptive editorial comments when it was nearing completion.

The cover photograph is reproduced with the permission of the Trustees of the Mitchell Library, State Library of New South Wales.